SPECIAL OPS

JOURNAL OF THE ELITE FORCES
& SWAT UNITS
VOL. 1

CONCORD
PUBLICATIONS COMPANY

A note from the editor

It is with great pleasure that we launch our first edition of "Special Ops". It is a journal that hopes to provide a glimpse into the missions, exploits and equipment of some of the world's fighting elite—from special forces commandos who strike far from their national frontiers to police tactical operators and EOD technicians who keep the streets of our towns and cities safe from heavily armed criminals and terrorists. Theirs is a world of danger and dedication, high-tech equipment and the basic surges of heroism. If there is one constant to their work it is that they exist as forces of last resort, to perform above and beyond the call of duty whenever summoned, no matter what the risk!

The end of the Cold War and the implementation of the New World Order may have helped to make the world safer from mutually-designed nuclear annihilation, but the collapse of communism has done little to make the world a safer place. Where the ideology of Lenin and Marx, and generous supplies of Soviet weapons, once brought revolution and civil war, the fervor of religious fundamentalism now fuels generations of holy warriors eager to enter into battle. They wage their war with suicide-bombings and aircraft hijackings, and the gory business of killing is viewed as nothing less than God's will. These forces are often well funded and protected by state-sponsorship and billions of petro-dollars. Collapsing frontiers have also proven to be a bonanza for organized crime entities whose thirst for power and profit, and penchant for unimaginable carnage in pursuit of their goals, have turned the streets of many of the world's most beautiful and peaceful cities into urban war zones.

Protecting the nations of the world from these often-invisible forces of evil has fallen to the special operations professionals—the men and women, who don the Nomex suits, Kevlar body armor and black balaclavas. Often the difference between a "job well done" and a massacre has been the instincts and skills of operators with fingers squeezing off quick bursts of MP5 fire, or having that right combination of training, courage and the indescribable right stuff needed to land on an enemy beachhead, free-fall from 10,000 feet, and slice a sentry's throat with a razor-sharp dagger. Increasingly, these battles are being waged on the streets of our cities—from Manhattan to Moscow, from Los Angeles to London.

In this, the first issue of "Special Ops" journal, we have profiled a unique and diverse selection of some of the world's busiest special operations forces—in both the military and law enforcement arena. Future issues hope to traverse the four corners of the globe to look at units that often survive in the enigmatic world of covert operations, dignitary protection, and SWAT call-outs; and cover the world of the operator, look at the equipment they carry, and study the battles they fight, and operations they execute.

Samuel M. Katz

"New York's Finest"
The NYPD's Emergency Service Unit In Action

Samuel M. Katz   **P 3**

U.S. Navy Special Boat Units (SBU)

Steven C. Bronson & Thomas B. Hunter

P 17

LEGIONNAIRES IN THE JUNGLE

Yves Debay   **P 27**

THE ISRAEL DEFENSE FORCES AIRBORNE CORPS

P 36   Steven Hartov

11th NL Airmobile Brigade

Walter Böhm   **P 47**

"Desert Commandos /Desert Aviators"

Jordanian Special Operations Capabilities Today

P 55   Samuel M. Katz

ISBN 962-361-636-8

printed in Hong Kong

"New York's Finest"

The NYPD's Emergency Service Unit In Action

Samuel M. Katz

P.O. Seth Gahr clutches his Ithaca-37 12-gauge shotgun.

ESU officers pose for the cameras with the back-drop of a bombed-out Harlem tenement.

Like most counter-terrorist operations, this one began with a whimper, rather than a bang. Like most counter-terrorist operations, the difference between back-slapping success and gut-wrenching failure hinged on skill, firepower, courage, and the almighty factor of divine luck. And, interestingly enough, it happened in, of all places, Brooklyn, New York.

On July 31, 1997, less than twenty-four hours after two suicide bombers blew themselves up in Jerusalem Mahane Yehuda Market, killing fifteen and wounding nearly a hundred, an Egyptian immigrant to the United States flagged down two police officers in Brooklyn terrified about something in his apartment building. Although he spoke little English, police were alarmed by his use of the word "Kaboom" every few sentences. An Arabic-speaking detective was brought in, as were federal agents assigned to the NYPD's Joint Terrorism Task Force. Once the informant was properly debriefed, the reason behind the fear in his voice became apparent—his two room-mates, Palestinian men in their twenties, were busy at work building two bombs that they planned to detonate in a

New York City subway station the following day. The two men, suspected to be Hamas terrorists infiltrated into the United States to commence a suicide-bombing spree that would kill hundreds, were less than twelve hours away from perpetrating their murderous suicidal rage.

In the vocabulary of American law enforcement, when a police department's heavy weapons unit is required to respond to a hostage-ordeal or heavily armed criminals, the acronym SWAT stands for **S**pecial **W**eapons **A**nd **T**actics, but in reality, the way police bureaucracies work, SWAT actually stands for **S**it, **W**ait **A**nd **T**alk. Police department bureaucracies are such in America that the hierarchy will often exhaust all peaceful means for ending a terrorist incident until they've reach an impasse and any further delays with a tactical solution might result in the loss of innocent lives. On this night in Brooklyn, though, there was no time for sitting, waiting and talking. The bombers had to be taken out, and done so in an expeditious and stealth-like manner. On the streets of Brooklyn, up against two suicide-bombers, there would be little room for error. New York City was lucky that night—it deployed an elite unit of

P.O. Pete Quinn readies his Ithaca-37 12-gauge shotgun prior to setting out on patrol.

ESU's XO (executive officer) Captain Ralph Pascullo takes aim with his Glock Model 19 9mm semiautomatic.

super-cops who were used to operating in the gray area of danger where second-chances were often luxuries that did not exist.

In New York, when heavy weapons are needed, the New York City Police Department (NYPD) calls upon the services of the Emergency Service Unit—its elite 400-man SWAT and rescue force. Trained as commandos, medics, SCUBA-divers and snipers, the men and women of the Emergency Service Unit had thought they had done and seen it all—from raiding drug factories, to protecting 150 world leaders at the fiftieth anniversary of the United Nations, to retrieving victims from the World Trade Center bombing, to searching for victims of the TWA 800 crash. They had never, though, come across suicide bombers prepared to kill thousands. When selecting the assault team, the Emergency Service Unit captain leading the operation selected only volunteers—only those without wives and kids were allowed to be the first through the door. After all, they'd have only seconds to locate and contain the bombers and secure the terrorists while the Bomb-Squad hurriedly defused the deadly devices. Any delay, any hesitation, or any obstacles, and the cops, the

terrorists, and the twenty people living in the building would be dead.

Racing toward the location in an unmarked van, the six-man entry team focused solely on the task at hand. They wore heavy Kevlar assault vests, heavy Kevlar Fritz-helmets and they carried automatic rifles and submachine guns. "If the bad guys wanted to challenge us," claimed one of the cops, "they were going to lose." Entering the building, the cops raced up two flights of stairs and, using the informant's key, gained silent entry into the apartment. With their weapons raised and fingers on the trigger, they slinked through the cramped flat awaiting what they feared most. Suddenly, one of the bomb-makers, twenty-two-year-old Lafi Khalil, lunged from behind a bed toward a black bag. He managed to pull two of the four ignition switches on the bomb before he was shot five times. His partner, twenty-three-year-old Gazil Ibrahim Abu Mezer then lunged for one of the cops, but he too was cut down by a hail of gunfire and critically wounded.

If the NYPD Emergency Service Unit cops hadn't acted so

Lieutenant Richard Greene, commander of the "A Team," aims down on his Glock 9mm.

During a protective security assignment for one of the defendants in the World Trade Center bombing, ESU officers secure a perimeter with the Heckler and Koch MP5s.

forcefully, so decisively, and so bravely, the two Palestinians could have detonated their devices and killed everyone in the building—themselves, the cops and the ten families that could not be evacuated. Had the NYPD's operators not acted so quickly, the terrorists might have managed to barricade themselves inside the location and take the twenty-odd residents of the apartment building hostage. "This business hinges on seconds," claims the NYPD captain who was forced to order his men into what many feared was certain death, "it's a race against time against men—and women—who are trained and determined to kill you before you can disrupt their plans. It's one hell of a way to make a living!"

In the twenty-five years since the Munich Olympic Massacres and the almost weekly hijackings of aircraft, ocean liners, buses and trains, hostage-rescue and counter-terrorism, like the operation in Brooklyn, has developed into a well-defined science. The men, and sometimes women, who have dedicated themselves to police special operations, live by the code of the impossible. They operate under the most desperate of conditions and perform their duties when lives hang in the balance and every second counts. They stand at the ready twenty-four-hours-a-day awaiting that call when they'll have to don their protective gear, grab their weapons, and stands only yards away from hard-core terrorists holding a group of innocent people hostage. They must have the patience of Solomon, the instincts of a seasoned detective, and be able to burst through a door and face the threat of bullets and explosives the moment the order of go has been issued. They must know when and who to shoot, and they must know who not to. They must be able to make individual decisions in the blinding flash of a diversionary device's blast, and operate as an integral element of a team where hand gestures replace the spoken language. They must not waiver and they must not fail. They don't get second chances and unless success is complete, their mission has resulted in innocents getting killed. While these cops aren't supermen and superwomen, the city they serve call upon them to perform super-human tasks of last resort and desperation. Welcome to the world of a select group of specialists who operate with the rush of adrenaline and the knowledge that seconds truly count. They are called upon to perform the impossible when the lives of innocent citizens hang in the balance and all that separates a hostage-taking situation from turning into a massacre is their skill, courage, and firepower. They explode into action, select their targets in a spilt-second of judgment and instinct, and are among the most superbly trained soldiers and policemen in the world today. They are the men that you would want to see bursting through the door with weapons ablaze if you were taken hostage. In New York City, that distinction belongs to ESU—the Emergency Service Unit.

"10-13" is the NYPD radio code for officer needs assistance, and every time the call for help goes out over the department's airwaves, hearts begin to pump faster, adrenaline begins to pump, and squad cars and response vehicle gun their engines and flash their lights and siren. But there is an old saying in the NYPD: "When a citizen needs help he calls a cop, when a cop needs help he calls ESU. The men and women of ESU are *the* elite unit of the New York City Police Department and, in essence, the city's last resort in time of crisis. Some in the department call the ESU officers "super cops" some call them E-men. They are jack-of-all-trades trained to be the department's tactical, or SWAT, entity capable of responding to a litany of tactical situations where firepower, negotiating skills and non-lethal means need to be employed. Yet ESU cops are also emergency medical technicians trained to administer life-saving treatment to the victims of any and all disasters, and they are craftsman and expert tool operators that can rescue trapped victims from overturned vehicles or blown up buildings with uncanny speed and remarkable resourcefulness.

If the streets of New York City can be considered a war-zone ripe in the madness of urban combat, then the officers of the NYPD's

P.O. Dan Donnelly aims his Heckler and Koch MP5.

While on a tactical training exercise, P.O. Vinny Martinez utilizes an R.E.P. as cover as he aims with his MP5.

Prior to a "hit" (the serving of a warrant) in Harlem, P.O. Eddie O'Neill readies his MP5.

P.O. (now Sgt.) John Politoski takes cover while aiming his Mini-14 5.56mm assault rifle.

P.O. Billy Pieszak of Eight-Truck in Brooklyn North cradles a Mini-14 with a laser aiming device inside the confines of the "big" truck.

P.O. Pete Tetukevich monitors a potentially high-threat individual with his M-24 7.62mm sniper rifle, while P.O. Ann-Margaret Lyons serves as observer.

Emergency Service Unit are the city's front line commandos and combat medics. While most police departments maintain small units of special weapons and tactics officers for high-risk situations, emergency rescue work is usually in the hands of Fire Departments or Fire-Rescue agencies. The New York City experience is different and, as a result, claims one former ESU lieutenant, in a city that has literally seen it all, in a police department that has coped with it all, ESU has done it all! If a building collapses in the TriBeca section of Manhattan, it is ESU officers that sift through the rubble and remove tons of debris to save trapped victims and retrieve the dead. If a precinct in the drug-plagued streets of South Jamaica, Queens, issues a warrant for a homicide suspect known to carry a 9mm, the officers of ESU, flak vests and MP5s, are summoned to gain entry to the suspect's apartments and "apprehend" him. A USAir jet plunges into the frigid waters of Flushing Bay following an aborted take-off from ice-covered LaGuardia airport, in a city-wide call-up for ESU whose officers don dry-suits and lunge into the ice-cold water to pull out twenty-four trapped passenger and crew, as well as retrieving the twenty-seven dead. A drunk subway motorman crashes his No. 6 train into a divider and forces the train to derail and partially overturn over the deadly electric currents of the Third Rail, and once again its the ESU that are called in to lift up the train and pull out seriously hurt passengers trapped by tons of steel and thousands of volts of juice. A driver is pinned down by his steering wheel and what is left of his car and it is the ESU that is summoned. A VIP visits the Big Apple and ESU sharpshooters, perched atop a rooftop amid the smoke-stacks and chimneys, peer through their M-24 rifles on counter-sniper duty. ESU, besides being the world's busiest tactical unit, is also the world's busiest rescue unit.

The Emergency Service Unit traces its creation to 1925 and the

An ESU sniper in action.

formation of a reserve force of officers who could be called on to perform "extraordinary" rescue assignments; many of these volunteers were also part-time carpenters, welders, riggers and electricians and the trucks they rode, modified fire-trucks, soon carried larger and more specified emergency equipment. Years later, life-saving gear was added to the trucks, with the cops sent to emergency medical training. The unit was also among the nation's first mobile tactical response force with what was once called the department's Firearms Battalion; as its officers carried Thompson submachine gun, the unit was also known by the daunting nickname of the "Machine Gun Squad." The unit eventually developed into a force called the Mobile Security Unit (MSU) that was tasked with its original mandate of responding to emergency situations such as wrecks and disasters, as well as backing up precinct cops on dangerous jobs that the lightly armed precinct officers were ill-equipped to handle. In the early 1970s the unit soon developed a counter-terrorist tactical role, especially involving hostage-rescue, following the 1972 Munich Olympic Massacre. At the time, few police forces possessed a special tactics and weapons unit that could deal with a hostage crisis, and few police forces knew how to deal with the rising tide of criminals armed with heavier firepower than the cops on the beat. With a rising heroin epidemic in the 1970s and an explosive crack situation in 1980s, however, ESU didn't have to wait until terrorists decided to strike before being deployed tactically. They became one of the busiest tactical response units in the world encountering a criminal element that was well armed and indiscriminate in their use of high-powered weapons.

Currently, ESU consists of approximately 400 officers (including bosses)—a small force considering the fact that with over 38,000 men under uniform, the NYPD is the largest municipal police force in the

An ESU sniper takes aim in Queens.

The big truck and some of the equipment it carries—this one belonging to Eight-Truck in Brooklyn North.

Sergeant John Boesch, of Nine-Truck, stands proudly in front of Eight-Truck in northern Brooklyn.

United States and the second largest in the world (next to the Tokyo Police). ESU falls under the command of the NYPD's Special Operations Division (SOD), a command that also controls aviation, harbor, mounted, street crime and highway units. ESU is divided into ten Trucks—or squads—spread out across the city's five boroughs; their quarters are always attached to an existing neighborhood precinct. ESU's city-wide responsibilities are follows: One-Truck is based in Lower Manhattan and responsible for the half of the island below 59th Street; Two-Truck, the "Jewel of Harlem," is responsible for Manhattan north of 59th Street; Three-Truck and Four-Truck are responsible for the Bronx; Five-Truck is in Staten Island; Six-Truck operates in Brooklyn South, Seven-Truck serves southeastern Brooklyn, and, Eight-Truck serves Brooklyn North; Nine-Truck and Ten-Truck are both responsible for the borough of Queens. Although each "Truck" has a distinctive piece of territory carved out for itself, large-scale situations and city-wide emergencies often warrant trucks to cross bridges and borough boundaries for back-up. This could range from a barricaded perpetrator "job" in Queens requiring back-up from the Bronx and Manhattan (along with their specialized vehicles), to city-wide disasters like the bombing of the World Trade Center on February 26, 1993, in which almost every unit in the city was rushed to lower Manhattan to search for and rescue victims trapped in the smoke-filled skyscraper.

An R.E.P. blocks traffic during a high-risk vehicular stop in northern Manhattan.

Few law enforcement units are tasked with as diverse and all-encompassing a list of assignments as is ESU. The description of their formal city-wide patrol and support functions include:

• **ROUTINE PATROL FUNCTION**: (a) patrol omnipresence, (b) summons issuance and arrests, (c) assist precincts in CPOP (Community Policing Program) efforts, (d) response to priority assignments and crimes in progress;

• **WARRANTS**: Search and arrest (a) assist in search for evidence and armed perpetrators, (b) apprehend violent felons, (c) assist in tactical planning or raid, (d) provide specialized weapons and heavy vests, (e) assist in search, removal of walls, flooring and structural modifications, especially narcotics cases, (f) provide entry into premises through battering rams, forced entry tools, secure doors; animal control (Pit Bulls, Dobermans, etc.), and (g) provide special equipment, entry tools, Hurst tools, hand tools, lighting.

• **SEARCHES**: (a) Crime scene searches, evidence searches (weapons and materials) and collection of same, difficult search areas, elevator shafts, duct work, venting systems, construction sited, sewers, manholes, street excavation, safeguarding crime scene, perimeter security and police lines, (b) perpetrator searches, provide heavy weapons and vests, secure perimeter, tactics for systematic/safe search, provide specialized equipment and expertise, (c) missing person searches/lost children and adults, special equipment and lighting and

During a HazMat job in Queens, units from Nine-Truck respond to the emergency.

difficult search areas (d) entry areas, access to rooftops and entry holes in floors walls and other locations.

• **EMOTIONALLY DISTURBED PERSONS** (EDPs): respond to all EDP runs, mental health removal orders, suicide attempts/jumpers, specialized equipment (Kevlar gloves, EDP bar), non lethal weaponry (Taser, Nova, water canon), restraining devices (Mesh blanket, Velcro straps), assist EMS in preparation for transport, develop tactical plans for approaching and restraining person with minimal injury to all involved. ESU officers are also trained in bridge and building rescue techniques and suicide prevention dialogue, and trained in robotics, and erecting a net and air bags.

• **BARRICADED PERPETRATOR/HOSTAGES**: establish and

SS!
ET
NO ACCESS! NO ACCESS!
WITHOUT HEAVY DUTY VEST & HELMET

NO ACCESS! NO ACCESS!
WITHOUT HEAVY DUTY VEST & HELMET

NO ACCESS! NO ACCESS!
WITHOUT HEAVY DUTY VEST & HELMET

During a barricaded-perp job in the South Bronx, an R.E.P. from Three-Truck blocks a city street.

One of ESU's two Peace-keeper armored cars.

secure inner perimeter, develop tactical plans, provide specialized weapons and heavy vests, assist hostage negotiation team, recovery of hostages, apprehension of hostage-takers, provide specialized equipment, bomb blankets, monitoring equipment, surveillance positions, observation teams, special weapons teams and Emergency Rescue Vehicles (E.R.V.s).

- **CRIME IN PROGRESS RESPONSES**: police officer shot, robbery in progress, shots fired, bank alarms/holdups,
- **OTHER EMERGENCIES**: water/ice rescues, disasters, sniper situation, riots/crowd control.
- **DIGNITARY PROTECTION**: The Emergency Service Unit is also the department's primary force in providing dignitary protection and VIP security—a monstrous task in a city as large and diverse as New York City. This includes presidential visits, national political leaders, visits from foreign heads of state, religious leaders and other dignitaries that require special security details and consideration. As New York City is a truly an international city and headquarters to the United Nations and various international financial institutions, these details are carried out virtually all year round. In performing these duties, ESU interacts and operates with State and Federal agencies, such as the U.S. Secret Service, the FBI, the New York State Police, and foreign security agencies. ESU supervisors and officers will work together with representatives to develop and formulate escape and rescue routes. In their dignitary protection role, ESU utilizes all its vehicles and equipment, including a Counter-Assault Team Vehicle (or "C.A.T. Car") to follow motorcades, and observation teams and counter-sniper marksman. ESU also provides additional security assistance in bomb-sweeps and motorcade security—a precarious undertaking on New York's grid-locked plagued streets and thruways. ESU officers provide additional tactical security to sensitive convoys heading through New York City, such as escorting dangerous felons

heading upstate to prison, and large shipments of narcotics being ferried out of the city to be destroyed upstate. Security details also involve the ESU counter-sniper team.

- **EXPLOSIVE DEVICES/BOMB SCARES**: ESU is also responsible for assisting the NYPD Bomb Squad in the event a suspicious package or device is located. ESU units will secure a safe perimeter and follow the "I.C.E." doctrine—**I**solate, **C**ontain and **E**vacuate. ESU officers will assist in the search for any reported device, and will then assist the Bomb Squad in its removal in either the Bomb Truck, or a total containment vessel. With the reemergence of the Unibomber, a serial bomber believed to operate out of the West Coast who was recently behind the murder of a New York City advertising executive in his home in New Jersey, calls of suspicious packages in the five boroughs have increase hundred-fold. At the height of the Unibomber hysteria, when ESU and the bomb-squad were following one call after another, a subway train in lower Manhattan was fire-bombed. In one very odd instance, when Bronx female officers were working undercover posing as prostitutes to arrest johns, a man driving a van with pipe bombs, cans crammed with black powder and a flame-thrower was arrested

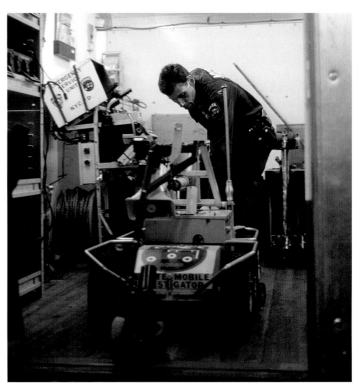

P.O. John D'Allara of Two-Truck readies the truck's robot from the R.M.I. truck during a barricade job in Harlem.

Summoned to the Bronx during a barricaded EDP job, ESU officers suit up in the back of the large truck.

Officers from Two-Truck respond to a fortified apartment and an EDP armed with a high-powered rifle inside a housing project in northern Manhattan.

After negotiations fail, the ESU entry team makes its move inside the apartment.

ESU executive officer Captain Ralph Pascullo confers with officers from Two-Truck during a barricaded perp job in Spanish Harlem.

and his vehicle and home searched by ESU and the Bomb Squad.

A "truck" is the ESU name for their quarters (as opposed to precinct) and it is also the force's main work-station, as the two types of vehicles the unit possesses are mini-command and mobile rescue platforms. The smaller ESU vehicle is the R.E.P or **R**adio **E**mergency **P**atrol, a cabin of emergency gear loaded on a 4x4 pickup. Each ESU Truck usually maintains three R.E.P.s and two are usually on patrol through the Truck's area of responsibility; they are known as the "Adam," "Boy," and "Charlie" cars. By performing roving patrols, R.E.P.s are in an excellent position to respond to emergencies requiring ESU expertise, such as "pin jobs," and tactical support for precinct officers responding to confirmed reports of shots fired or robbery in progress. The R.E.P. carries a little bit of all the unit's emergency rescue equipment, protective body armor, though the heaviest bit of firepower carried is the Ithaca 12-gauge shotgun. The equipment it carries includes:

- **General Equipment -** two high intensity portable lights, two gas masks, two sound barriers, two goggles, one jumper cables, one slim Jim, two heavy vests, two construction helmets, two ballistic helmets, two ballistic shields, ballistic blanket, battering ram, two shotguns and ammunition, two batons, two hand-lights, HazMat book, rescue harness, Larakus belts with carabiners, webbing, and binoculars.
- **Non-Lethal Weaponry/EDP Equipment -** Tasers and darts, Nova stun device and pole, water canon, shepherds crook, Kevlar stainless steel gloves, chemical mace, pepper gas, EDP bar, mesh restraining blanket, Velcro restraining straps, 15 inch chain handcuffs, and plastic shield.
- **Hurst Tools -** gas motor Jaws, cutters, chains, gas can aviation tips, ram, 26' hoses.
- **Pneumatic Tools -** Pneumatic saw kit, paratech air guns.
- **Air Bags -** air bags three sizes, air bag bottles, air bag regulators, train kit, assorted chocks, cribbing.
- **Gas Powered Chain Saw -** Sthil chain saw with tool kit, spare chain, fuel.
- **Scuba Gear -** two Viking dry suits, two open-cell thermal underwear, two AGA masks with regulators, two Scuba tanks and backpack, two sets fins, gloves, knives, compass, two weight belts, two BCD vests, two sets rescue line, two underwater lights, two 150' polyprop lines.
- **Tools and Other Equipment -** bolt cutters large and small, wire

cutters, ring cutter, lock buster, sledge hammer, haligan tool, ax, bow saw, come-along tool, small Haligan, tool box, hack saw, pry bar, gas key, crow bar, "J" hook, assorted small tools, lock cylinder tool, two "J" chains, chain with hooks, radiac kit, Kelly tool, lanterns, dosimeters, isolation kit, flares, circle cord, reflective tape, oil.
- **First Aid Kit -** resuscitator, two O2 tanks, demand valve, suction, assistant masks, Cervical collars, K.E.D extrication, spare O2 bottles, body bag. D.B.-45, sterile water, O.B. kit, burn kit, stokes basket, scoop stretcher, folding stretcher, backboard - long and short, blankets, assorted splints, disposable body bags, canvas body bags, DB-45 deodorizer.
- **Other Equipment -** Two Scott packs, two 1 hour bottles, "B" suit, rubber gloves, electrical gloves, magnet, elevator and electronic kit, two waders, exposure suit, 50' Line and life ring, Kapock vests, work line 1/2: work line assorted, life line, dog noose, animal control kit, "Hot Stick," gas masks, goggles and work gloves, reflective tape, sound barriers, 16" extension ladder.
- **Fire Extinguishers -** One water, one dry chem. one CO2.
- **Vehicle Stabilization Equipment -** Four 6x6 hardwood chocks, four 3x3 chocks, assorted wedges, chocks, shoring and cribbing.

The larger of the two vehicles is the "Truck," a hulking $250,000 vehicle ($1,000,000 when fully equipped) the size of a garbage truck that are usually despatched to large-scale jobs and as a back-up for the R.E.P.s. If the equipment carried inside the R.E.P. can be considered mind-boggling, than the multitude of rescue and tactical gear would appear to be enough to equip a small police force. The "Truck's" equipment inventory consists of the following:
- **Gas Powered Chain Saws -** Sthil chain saw, with tool, kit, spare chain, fuel, K-1200 saw with: wood blades, steel blades, masonry blades, tool kit and fuel.
- **Electric Power Tools -** Reciprocating saw, Circular saw, High-tork drill, all above tools have spare blades and bits of all sizes.
- **Radiac Equipment -** Two Geiger counters, four docemeters, twenty film badges.
- **Electrical and Lighting Equipment -** Four 100' electrical reels, four 1000 watt portable lights, two 500 watt portable lights, two 1000 watt light towers, two 4000 watt light towers, assorted adapters and plugs,

two multiport junction boxes.

- **Hand Tools -** Forty piece tool box, two sets bolt cutters large and small, sledge hammers 5 lb. and 10 lb., Haligan tools large and small, two pike head axes, two flat head axes, three bow saws small, medium, large, carpenter saws, pry bars 12", 18", 24," lock buster (duck bill), Hydraulic bolt cutters, "Rabbit Tool," various gas and utility shut, off keys, shovels, trench, spade, flat, various hydrant wrenches, lock puller, "K" tool kit, Kelly tool, grading hooks, hot stick, assorted spikes and nails, rakes and brooms, 24' extension ladder, pike polls, closet ladder 12', portable vise, winch (come-a-long), assorted hand tools.
- **Truck Mounted Equipment -** Five Ton winch, Air compressor, 24 KW Generator, light towers, PA radio system, spot and flood lights.
- **Cutting Torches -** One Caldo torch with rods, one oxyacetylene back pack, assorted tips 10' hoses.
- **First Aid Equipment -** Major trauma kit, Back boards, cervical collars, resuscitator, spare 02 bottles, K.E.D.s, blankets, assorted splints, burn kit, stokes basket, scoop stretcher.

- **Pneumatic Tools -** pneumatic saw kit (wizard), paratech air gun, Pneumatic jacking bags, Five sized, control kit, pneumatic air chisel.
- **Hydraulic Tools -** Porto-power kit ten ton, Hurst tools- Hurst 5000 gas motor, Hurst electric motor, Hurst)-150 cutters, Hurst model 32-B, Hurst model 26 champ, Hurst model 16 ram, Hurst model 30 ram.
- **Specialized Equipment -** metal detector, Train kit, two 10 ton jacks, hydraulic bolt cutters, electric jack hammer, line gun, Porta-lights (hand lights).
- **Heavy Weapons and Ammunition -** Ithaca pump shotgun, Heckler and Koch MP5 9mm sub machine guns, Ruger Mini-14 5.56mm assault rifles, two 9mm Semi-automatic pistol, one Ruger Mini-14 Laser sighted rifle, two Federal 37mm tear gas projectile gun.
- **Tactical Equipment -** six ballistic helmets, six ballistic vests, one body bunker ballistic shield, two ballistic barrier blankets, one forced entry door ram, six M.S.A. gas masks with filters, one Kwik - View mirror, one spotting scope.
- **Rope -** two 200' 1/2 life line, one 220' 5/8" life line, 100' 5/8 work line manil., 100' 1/2" work line manil., 100' 3/8 work line manil., 500' 1/4"

Racing toward a "hit," P.O. Vinny Martinez mans the ballistically-protective Body Bunker shield.

While ESU heads in through the front door on a narcotics location, an NYPD narcotics detectives covers a rear exit with his Glock 9mm.

During a warrant, an officer races through the door in support of the line of cops that raced through the bolted shut door of the drug-house.

As an officer with a flash-light searches for suspects that might be hiding, another officer covers his back with his MP5.

With the smoke still lingering from the detonated diversionary device, officers prepare to hit another apartment in a Manhattan North crack house.

ESU officers enter a Bronx drug location during a "hit."

Sergeant Juan Garcia of Two-Truck leads a hit into the first floor of a Harlem drug location.

After a job well done, ESU officers from the Bronx depart a hit Harlem drug location.

ploy-prop. cord, four Morrisey life belts, two rescue harness.

- **HazMat Kit**
- **S.C.B.A. Equipment -** two SCBA Scott-packs in case, six spare 60 minutes bottles, 6 spare 30 minutes bottles.
- **Hydraulic Tools -** Hurst hydraulic manual pump, post support plate, two chains with clevis hooks, two clevis links, clevis pins, assorted tips, fuel, oil, two spare 16' hoses.
- **Vehicle Stabilization Equipment -** six 6x6 hardwood chocks, six 4x4 hardwood chocks, assorted wedges, chocks, shoring and cribbing.
- **Fire Extinguishing Equipment -** two pressurized water extinguisher, Dry Chemical ext., two CO2 ext., two 50' rolls 1 1/2" fire hose with nozzles.
- **Elevator and Electrical Equipment -** Elevator and electric kit.
- **Non-Lethal weaponry/EDP -** Taser and darts, Nova stun device and pole, water canon, shepherds crook, Kevlar stainless steel gloves, chemical mace, pepper gas, EDP bar, mesh restraining blanket, Velcro restraining straps, 15 inch chain handcuffs, plastic shield.
- **Water Rescue Equipment -** six Kapock vests, two ring buoy's with 80' rope, two shepherds hooks, exposure suits, two sets waders, 4 man inflatable raft (AVON) with oars, one 4hp outboard engine.
- **SCUBA Gear -** two Viking dry suits, two open-cell thermal underwear, two AGA masks with regulators, four 80 cu. ft. scuba tanks, two B.C.D. vests, two sets fins, gloves, knives and compass, four Darrel-Allen underwater lights, two sets of 150' water rescue lines, two sets of weight belts.
- **Animal Control Equipment -** two dog noose's Animal control kit.
- **Other Equipment -** Assorted Rigging equipment block and tackle.

Other vehicles in the ESU fleet include a bomb truck, a total containment vessel, a truck for the unit's three "Remote Mobile Investigators"; mobile light generators; Construction Accident Response Vehicles; Jumper Response Vehicle (Air Bags); a Hazardous material Decontamination Trailer; Generator Trucks; Photo Observation Vehicle; a Temporary Headquarters Vehicle; and, two snowmobiles. Among the more specialized ESU vehicles are two M75 APCs known as E.R.Vs for **E**mergency **R**escue **V**ehicles, which are used primarily to evacuate a wounded officer or civilian in an areas under fire. Recently, ESU has obtained two Peace-keepers and has already deployed them in jobs involving barricaded perpetrators holding hostages.

Sometimes, an R.E.P. can patrol a stretch of one of the city's five borough's and not encounter a single emergency call—not even a summons. In the R.E.P., ESU cops monitor the precinct, division and SOD radios in an audible juggle meant to listen in on possible jobs that they might eventually get called to, and gain a few precious seconds in response time in reaching the scene.

As they are the only SWAT-like unit in the United States and the world tasked with emergency rescue work, ESU officers possess a unique perspective when handling their day-to-day duties. According to Lieutenant Bob Sobocienski, a highly-decorated unit supervisor with twenty-six years on the job, "Our main purpose is to save lives! We are different than other tactical units in other departments because deep in the back of our minds we are always in our rescue mode." The protection of human life is an all-important, and sometimes unheralded aspect of the unit's daily work that the public never hears about unless they themselves are rescued by ESU officers.

As suspects are cuffed, an ESU officer guards the inner perimeter with his MP5 9mm submachine gun.

During a hit in Harlem's notorious 2-8 Precinct, A-Team training officer P.O. Derek Dunston ensures outer perimeter safety for the remainder of the team inside.

There isn't a major emergency—criminal or accident—in New York City that escapes the attention—and desperately needed services—of ESU. In terms of rescue work, ESU is tasked with saving lives in every part of the city under any and all circumstances. In the poor communities of the city, in the housing projects, ESU is often summoned to rescue youngsters (or retrieve their bodies) after a game of "elevator surfing," while along the highways surrounding the affluent Upper East Side of Manhattan, ESU crews are routinely summoned to "53-Pins-With-Injuries," traffic accidents where expensive cars are often wrapped around bits of highway with their drivers trapped inside. ESU officers treat Pin Jobs as if they were embarking on a "hit"—with speed, determination and the utmost professionalism. Upon arriving at the scene of a Pin Job, officer race from their R.E.P.s and Trucks, and remove the necessary life-saving extrication gear the job will require with record speed. Each ESU officers is certified by Hearst Tool Manufacturers in the operation of the "Jaws of Life" and other cutting and prying attachments which adapt to the specialized gear. The objective in extricating a victim from being pinned in a vehicle is to safely remove the parties while not exacerbating any existing wounds or injuries, and then providing immediate first-aid trauma care to stabilize the injured party until they can be transported by ambulance to hospital. Some ESU officers, like the unit's EMT instructor Tommy Rowe, become full-fledged battlefield medics at emergency scenes; they will refer to the injured party as "patient" rather than victim. It should be noted that ESU is, perhaps, the sole specialized emergency police unit—be it rescue or tactical—that can boast an M.D. in its ranks (Sergeant Vic Politi, recently promoted to the rank of lieutenant is one such a remarkable individual), as well as a registered nurse (P.O. Cliff Allen of One-Truck).

In 1996, the last year that complete records were kept, ESU

responded to an incredible 13,241 vehicular accidents and 3,450 non-vehicular accidents. Non-vehicular accidents can be anything—and in New York City everything—from gaining entry to a disabled individuals apartment so that medical care can be administered to use rope and a Stokes basket to lower a 700lb woman down five flights of stairs so that she can be rushed to the hospital. Some rescue work has been unique and bizarre—it has ranged from little children getting their hands stuck in meat grinders, to adults, in the city's more colorful locations, needing to have body parts extricated from the gamut of mechanical devices. Some rescue work, however, is truly incredible and illustrates ESU's special skills, training and equipment. Virtually all ESU personnel are SCUBA-qualified, making the unit the largest underwater rescue and tactical force outside the U.S. Navy SEALs. In two instances in the past decade, ESU officers have ventured into the icy waters of Flushing Bay to race against the clock and pull survivors and victims out of two USAir jets attempting to take-off from LaGuardia Airport in Queens that ended up in the water, and they have sailed to the southern coast of Long Island in search of bodies—and evidence—in the wake of the July 17, 1996, crash of TWA Flight 800.

Besides being one of the world's largest single purchasers of rescue and life-saving gear, ESU's knowledge and expertise has been used around the globe. When Hurricane Hugo pummeled the island of Puerto Rico, an ESU team was en route to the battered island commonwealth, on a military transport, within hours of the devastating winds and waves; ESU officers, beyond searching for victims, helped fix running water to many of the island's residents. At their training facility inside a hangar at Floyd Bennet Field in Brooklyn, emergency medical, construction and recovery gear sits inside a sealed container awaiting deployment *anywhere* in the world. Following the April 19, 1995 bombing of the

P.O. Eddie Torres administers aid to a drowning victim during a rescue job in the Central Park reservoir.

Alfred P. Murrah Federal Building in Oklahoma City, a twenty-man contingent of ESU officers, an element of the FEMA (Federal Emergency Management Agency) Urban Search and Rescue Program (also consisting of firefighters and EMS medical technicians), was summoned for duty in Oklahoma City. Having sifted through the destruction inside the World Trade Center, the twenty-man ESU contingent thought it was prepared for what they found in Oklahoma. They were wrong. NYTF-1, as the force was known, worked twelve-hour shifts inside the rubble-filled shell of the federal building in a desperate, though highly professional, search for survivors. Unfortunately, there were no survivors to be found—only corpses.

One sensitive ESU responsibility is the handling of what is known in the vernacular as an "EDP"—an Emotionally Disturbed Person. It can arguably be said that New York is a city full of nuts, but EDPs are not just jaded New Yorkers disgruntled about dirty streets and over-crowded subway cars. These individuals are threats to themselves and others. They are wacky drug fiends, psychopaths on Angel Dust, and those who just want to off themselves. Sometimes these calls are handled by the first sight of a patrol car and a flashing light, other times the ESU truck can't get to the scene fast enough. ESU officers are specifically trained to handled emotionally disturbed individuals. They have some psychological training, and a lot of instruction in using electronic immobilizers that stun and sedate an EDP; they are also expert in using special rope and net systems to subdue and harness an individual who needs to be in a straight jacket for a while. As is departmental policy, non-lethal means need to be employed in handling an EDP—these can range from pepper spray and taser guns, to water cannons and metal poles. When handling an EDP, however, ESU officers don body armor and Fritz helmet before leaving their truck, and one officer brings his 12-gauge shotgun just in case.

Many EDPs, the despondent and the depressed, will often climb buildings or bridges and threaten to jump in a desperate final appeal for help. When the call for a jumper is received over the precinct or division radio, it is ESU that is raced to the scene. Expert ropesmen, ESU cops ties in to a building's roof when inching their way closer to someone threatening to jump; if the jumper goes down, the officers are determined not to be taken with them. Handling a jumper is a precarious endeavor and no two jobs are the same. Most jumpers use the ledges of buildings to showcase their desire to end it all, others prefer bridges and have climbed to incredible heights in order to jump or warrant them being saved.

While rescue work is a unique—and cherished—aspect of the ESU

trade, it is the tactical back-up that they provide to their brother and sister officers on the beat that is the bread and butter of their existence. In 1996, ESU performed over 2,500 tactical actions, including nearly 1,000 barricaded perpetrators and hostage situations. These tactical jobs involved suiting up and deploying with heavy-firepower; some jobs lasted as little as thirty minutes, others have lasted up to sixteen hours. Tactically speaking, the NYPD ESU is as professional, skilled and battle-tested as they come. Although they have trained with a variety of law-enforcement and military agencies to develop and hone their skills, it is the lessons learned on the streets of the city that is the guiding force behind the tactics ESU uses on jobs. Caution is the catchword of every tactical deployment, and every possible. ESU's primary objective in all its tactical work—especially hostage situations—is that deadly force is a last resort. "We'd rather bore you to death than shoot you," boasts Lieutenant Bob Sobocienski, "the term acceptable casualties is not in our dictionary. Maybe its because we are also a rescue unit dedicated to saving lives, but we will do our utmost not to use deadly force." A deliberate series of command checks-and-balances provides a built-in mechanism to make sure that when ESU goes through a door with weapons at the ready, that all other options have been exhausted.

When lethal force is required, ESU is more than adequately equipped to meet any threat encountered. Most ESU cops carry the Glock Model 19 9mm semi-automatic pistol; a long haul from the old .38s NYPD cops used to carry. Glocks and Beretta 92Ds fitted with flash-lights (for use by tactical point men carrying the Body Bunker) are carried on the truck and used for "hits." The unit's principal 9mm submachine gun is the Heckler and Koch MP5 A3 complete with HK94 tactical forearm with built-in light. The unit's primary assault rifle is the American-produced Ruger Mini-14 5.56mm assault rifle (an NYPD favorite), and the shotgun carried in R.E.P.s, patrol cars and supervisor vehicles is the Ithaca Model 37 12-gauge shotgun. The ESU counter-sniper fields the Remington's M-24 7.62mm system.

Warrants and tactical entries is the bread-and-butter of ESU's heavy-weapon's work. They have the training to gain entry to locations that have been fortified and booby-trapped, they have the specialized entry tools (from hydraulic spreaders known as "Rabbit Tools" to the hard-hitting sledge-hammers and battering rams), they have the weapons to get the job done, and they have the courage to go through a door opposite a murder suspect or a narcotics dealer armed with an AK-47 or a MAC-10. For the most part, warrants are handled by the officers serving in one of the ten trucks—a precinct in a truck's territory will receive a warrant and the precinct commander (or commander of a narcotics, Street Crimes or homicide unit) will then contact ESU. Because ESU officers are only

One of the aerial assets of NYPD that often works hand-in-hand with ESU—an NYPD Aviation Unit Bell 206 Jet Ranger.

An ESU officer rappels from the Roosevelt Island tramway to the East River below during emergency rescue training.

human and can only be in one place at one time, and because it is impossible to respond to a hostage situation when the officers on a truck are trying to separate a man from his over-turned truck, ESU has created tactical teams that are on permanent stand-by status for the execution of tactical warrants. Known by its nickname of the "A-Team," for "Apprehension Tactical Team," two squads are dedicate solely to full-time tactical work and assisting the precinct captains (as well as federal agencies working in the city) in gaining a tactical entry to a location in order to serve a warrant. The "A-Team," especially the squad made up of officers pooled together from the various trucks on a rotated three-month tour, is a cohesive unit that utilizes and maximizes a tactical team concept in gaining entry to and securing a location. Unlike the other ESU squads who deploy from their R.E.P.s and Trucks, the "A-Team" often reaches their objective discreetly in unmarked C.A.T. cars, typical SWAT bread-trucks, and other nondescript vehicles.

Protective Security work also provides ESU with an enormous workload of tactical work—VIP security is a monstrous task in a city as important as New York. This VIP work includes presidential visits, national political leaders, visits from foreign heads of state, religious leaders and other dignitaries that require special security details and consideration; as New York City is a truly international city and headquarters to the United Nations and various international financial institutions, these details are carried out virtually all year round. ESU routinely interacts and operates with State and Federal agencies, such as the U.S. Secret Service, the FBI, Marshals Service, the New York State Police, and foreign security agencies. ESU supervisors and officers will work together with representatives to develop and formulate escape and rescue routes. In their dignitary protection role, ESU utilizes all its vehicles and equipment, including a Counter-Assault Team Vehicle (or "C.A.T. Car") to follow motorcades, and observation teams and counter-sniper marksman. ESU also provides additional security assistance in bomb-sweeps and motorcade security—a precarious undertaking on New York's grid-locked plagued streets and thruways. In October 1995, ESU found itself involved in the two largest VIP security details in the city's—and nation's—history. The first "important" visitor requiring a unique ring of protection was Pope John Paul II. ESU, supplementing FBI, Secret Service, and other federal law enforcement, was out in force to safeguard the pontiff during his busy itinerary in New York City, from protecting him during mass in Central Park and Aqueduct Raceway, to an impromptu stroll to greet worshippers on Fifth Avenue outside St. Patrick's Cathedral. The second detail was, according to one very experienced NYPD sergeant, "the mother of all operations." For the fiftieth anniversary of the United Nations, 152 world leaders converged on New York City for five days of speeches, meetings, celebrations,

ESU training officers train in the art of deploying from a helicopter's landing skids at the unit's training facility at Floyd Bennet Field, Brooklyn.

gridlock and a massive security nightmare. It was the largest protective operation in United States law enforcement history, involving every federal law enforcement agency. For the NYPD, it was a massive security headache. ESU officers served twenty-hour days to maintain the vigilant ring of security surrounding such high-profile security risks as President Clinton, Cuban Premier Fidel Castro, Jordan's King Hussein, PLO Chairman Yasir Arafat, and, ominously, Israeli Prime Minister Yitzhak Rabin.

ESU is the elite of the NYPD, and the hardest—and most sought after—unit to get into. Service in ESU is on a strictly volunteer basis, and the waiting list to get in or even be considered for the unit is 1,500 names long. To be eligible to volunteer, an officer must have five years on the job with an exemplary service record, pass a psychological and physical examination, as well as an extensive oral examination. ESU is primarily looking for officers with additional skills, such as carpenters, electricians and craftsman who can combine the tactical aspects of the job with the rescue role; officers with SCUBA or military skills are also recruited and sought. Much of the recruitment is done via word of mouth and recommendations. The actual training, called the Specialized Training School (STS), lasts sixteen weeks and consists of everything from the A-Zs of tactical assaults with the MP5, to the underground labyrinth of city power lines. The curriculum includes:
- Bridge and building rescue techniques (including talking down a jumper and pulling one in)
- Vehicle and train accidents and building collapse extrication
- Rigging and Line techniques

ESU officer train with the M75, known as the ERV.

- Welding and burning
- First aid as first responders
- The operation of power rescue tools
- Elevator and escalator emergencies and rescues
- Animal control systems (in NYC, a potpourri of "animal jobs" from pitbulls, to wild raccoons and coyotes)
- Water rescue techniques
- Helicopter rescue, rappel
- Recognition of bombs and improvised explosive devices
- Transportation of bombs and explosive devices
- Recognition and rescue relative to hazardous material (HazMat)
- Operation of specialized vehicles
- Dignitary protection and escorts
- Specialized police apprehension and hostage-rescue tactics
- The handing of EDPs
- Use of chemical agents
- Use of self-contained breathing apparatus
- Use of auxiliary electrical generators and lighting equipment
- Handling of electrical and gas emergencies
- Aircraft emergencies
- Forcible entry techniques
- Hazardous materials
- Department of Corrections procedures
- Crime Scene Investigations
- High-rise structure rescues
- Torch and welding procedures

Other specialized training include one week of Emergency Psychological Technician Certification Course; a two week special weapons certification course; and three day remote tactics (robotics) course; a one day non-lethal weapons course (the Taser gun, pepper mace and water cannon); a two week scuba certification course known as PADI (Professional Association of Diving Instructors) includes basic and advances certification, dry suit and search and recovery special certification; and, a three week emergency medical technician (EMT) certification course. Tactical training is conducted at the ESU training facility (and headquarters) at Floyd Bennet Field, Brooklyn, and specialized tactical training is conducted annually (and sometimes three times a year) at Camp Smith, an army post and training camp along the Hudson River in upstate New York. At Camp Smith, ESU officers are able to practice their rappelling and fast-rope techniques (courtesy of a 300-foot high cliff); live fire TAC house where entry skills can be honed up and mastered anew; helicopters assault techniques; VIP protection exercises with the C.A.T. car; and, recovery exercises with the E.R.V.

On November 9, 1997, the NYPD, the New York City Office of Emergency Management, the FBI and several other agencies as well as elements of the New York Fire Department carried out "Operation Ice," a large-scale training exercise meant to simulate the effects and decontamination woes of a section of lower Manhattan hit by a terrorist bomb filled with chemical and biological agents. The drill, in which ESU and its HazMat teams were at the forefront, was a direct result of the Sarin attack on the Tokyo subway, and recent bombings in Oklahoma City and the Middle East. With the streets of Manhattan simulating ground-zero, ESU crews wearing spaceman-like hazardous material suits located the devices, and proceeded to treating the contaminated area and contaminated victims with speed and determination. Many view such a scenario as terrific and utterly unfathomable. But the NYPD is not a department that leaves much for chance, and ESU is a city that has turned the unthinkable into yet another chapter in its long and proud history. After all, whether it is the routine or the unthinkable, ESU remains at the ready to provide its expert skills and unflinching courage to handle any and all emergencies.

The World's Busiest Dignitary Protection Unit

ESU Executive Officer Captain Ralph Pascullo greets President Clinton during a visit to New York City. (Courtesy: R.P.)

" In 1995, the NYPD proved itself to be the most vital, innovative, effective, and forward thinking police department in the nation, if not the world. The Papal visit and the UN's fiftieth anniversary showcased your skills. You rose to an enormous challenge, and you made it look easy. It was a textbook demonstration in how to manage large crowds and maintain blanket security." Former Police Commissioner William J. Bratton, in the Sept./Oct. Issue of the NYPD Magazine, "Spring 3100"

There are few cities on the planet like New York City. An international center for commerce, communications, politics and entertainment, New York City is an ever-bustling metropolis that literally "never sleeps." And, it is also *the* city that is almost always on the itinerary of every president, prime minister, prince, or premier visiting North America. New York City receives more VIP visits than any other city in the United States, and the world for that matter—no other city, after all, has the United Nations, Wall Street and the Broadway theaters in its confines. Each VIP visit requires security, some more than others, while some demand unprecedented tactical vigilance.

As the chief VIP/Dignitary Protection team in New York City, ESU has become an international trend-setter in the tactical application of security to visiting world leaders. From occasional visits by such sensitive figures as Israeli Prime Minister Benjamin Netanyahu and U.S. President Bill Clinton, to rarer, though frantic, visits to the city by PLO Chairman Yasir Arafat and Cuban Premier Fidel Castro, ESU has handled them all. Such high-profile visits demand that ESU deploy officers, in full assault gear, MP-5s and Mini-14s in hand, inside hotels and banquet halls, counter-sniper teams on roof-tops, and CAT (counter-attack) cars on motorcades. According to one State Department Bureau of Diplomatic Security official, "These super cops afford us a ring of armor around all of our details."

ESU's greatest dignitary protection challenge came in October 1995 when, in the span of three weeks, the unit was pressed with a life-time's worth of VIP protection work. In October, Pope John Paul II visited New York and, two weeks later, as did 152 world leaders who attended the 50th anniversary of the United Nations. With a city full of threats, targets and a force of only 400 officers, ESU was the focal point of providing security to the pilgrimage of dignitaries visiting New

York City—a roster that included President Clinton, British Prime Minister John Major, Israeli Prime Minister Yitzhak Rabin, Jordan's King Hussein, PLO Chairman Yasir Arafat and even Cuban Premier Fidel Castro. For each and every of the 152 leaders that would assemble, there was at least one group who would want to assassinate them. No politician lived in an enemy-free society. What better place to knock-off a world leader than in New York. What better way to embarrass the United States of America? As is the case with most ESU operations, the frantic weeks of October 1995 ended without incident—although two reported attempted on the life of Cuban Premier Fidel Castro were deterred by the infrangible veil of Emergency Service Unit protection. In fact, in reflecting on the wild and incredible two weeks in October 1995, perhaps Special Agent in Charge Brian Gimlett, the United States Secret Service's man in New York City, said it best when he was quoted as saying, "I have supervised security efforts around the world and can honestly say that only this city and this police department is capable of hosting events of this magnitude."

"No other police unit in the world could have ever pulled off such an endeavor with such professionalism, spirit and innovative," claimed a visiting Israeli Police official to New York City during the operation. "In fact," he went on to say, "If the NYPD is the sword that protects the citizens of the city, then ESU is the razor-sharp tip of the blade."

An ESU counter-assault team deploys from its CAT car during a protective service assignment for the Cuban foreign minister.

An ESU CAT car races through Manhattan traffic.

U.S. Navy Special Boat Units (SBU)

Steven C. Bronson & Thomas B. Hunter

A 30' RIB off the coast of Sardinia, Italy. Joint operations and training. (U.S. Navy)

Overview

The U.S. Navy's Special Boat Units trace their history back to the "Brown Water Navy" of the Vietnam War. During this period, the U.S. Navy placed great emphasis on the construction of super-carriers, guided missile cruisers and other large, deep water vessels. And while these ships played an important role in the war, the Navy soon realized that such massive vessels were inappropriate in the prosecution of guerrilla warfare. Tactics required an entirely different approach in order to reach up into the enemy strongholds. The Vietcong (VC) used the thousands of miles of rivers and waterways for a variety of purposes, including resupply, transportation of wounded, war-tax collection, and troop deployments. It was soon realized that in order to halt these vital activities, it was imperative to develop and deploy not only small, shallow draft boats but also train their crews in small boat and special operations tactics. The result of this was the formation in 1963 of Boat Support Unit One, a component of the Naval Operations Support Group. This action spawned a number of wholly new and specialized units, such as the River Patrol Force and Mobile Riverine Force. During the course of the war, these predecessors to today's Special Boat Units chalked up an impressive operational record and drastically reduced the enemy's fighting capability on waterways once prohibited to conventional naval operations.

Today, SBU supports a wide range of special operations activity. These units are organized, trained, and equipped to operate a variety of surface combatant craft in both coastal and riverine environments. SBU consists of NSW (Naval Special Warfare) active and reserve fleet personnel. The craft most frequently employed are offshore, open-water, fast patrol boats and shallow-draft riverine patrol craft. Yet, as the majority of SEAL operations are carried out via surface craft, and not subsurface, the importance of the Special Boat Units cannot be overstated.

Training

Prospective members of the Special Boat Units must undertake a difficult training course, known formally as Special Warfare Craft Crew-member (SWCC). The SWCC is considered "high risk" by the U.S. Navy and stresses the development of such disciplines as small boat operations, weapons training, and other necessary skills. SBU training is generally considered to consist of three phases. In the first, each class of between eighteen and thirty sailors (some classes have been as low as eleven) will receive nine weeks of fundamental training in craft operation. They'll come out designated basic combatant craft crew members. Next, they'll spend up to a year in intense tactical training while serving with an operational special boat unit at Little Creek, Virginia, San Diego, New Orleans or Panama. It is then, as members of ten-to-fifteen men detachments, ten men Mk.V SOC (Special Operations Craft) crews, or fourteen-to-eighteen men mobile support crews, that the real training begins.

Prior to arriving at SWCC, each candidate will have undergone an interview by his Commanding Officer, be screened by his command physical fitness coordinator, interviewed by the local NSW recruiter or assigned representative (or a Chief Petty Officer from the SWCC community). He also must have been recommended by his Commanding Officer and submit a request for assignment to SWCC school. Once accepted, all SWCC candidates must pass an entrance physical fitness

A 30' RIB returning from the beach, where it dropped off SOF personnel. (U.S.Navy)

A 24' RIB towing a CRRC (Combat Rubber Raiding Craft). (U.S. Navy)

24' RIB maneuvering in tight quarters. One of the many facets of the RIB. (U.S. Navy)

test, consisting of a one-mile timed run, 500-yard timed swim, timed push ups, and sit ups.

During the students training at SWCC, the run distances increase, and the swim times and distances also increase. Discipline is stressed, and infractions are corrected with reminders, which at SWCC means harsh physical exercise. Swims in the bay after the students are comfortable in the pool followed by swims in the open ocean in order to prepare the students for work in the open ocean. Although swimming is not as significant a part of a SWCC crewman's job as it is for operators in the SEALs, they will often find themselves far out to sea in small craft, or deep in the jungles miles up a river. Because of this, though, they must be

A 24' RIB, slightly disguised for the E.J. Williams Building Dedication. BMC (Ret), Medal of Honor Recipient, E. J. Williams, was honored on July 17, 1997, when SBU- 20's new building was named in his honor. E. J. Williams is the U.S. Navy's most highly decorated enlisted man. (U.S. Navy)

RIBs underway for another day of training and exercises. (U.S. Navy)

adept in the water, in the event their craft is disabled or destroyed.

All SWCC personnel need to be physically fit in order to respond to the everyday requirements of the job, and still have adequate strength and endurance in reserve to effectively respond to an emergency. The ability to respond in an emergency is increased incrementally as physical fitness levels are increased. Runs on the beach are part of SWCC students training. Not nearly as much as their NSW brethren going through the grueling BUD/S course, but they all reside in the same quarters and physical fitness training is conducted everyday with some days spent at the pool and other days on the beach for a run. Keeping in mind that a physically fit person is more alert and apt to retain more, SWCC students normally score high on all tests. Many classroom sessions are actually taught while handling the equipment, or boats they will soon be using for their final training exercises before they can graduate. These boats may be tied next to the pier, on a trailer for ease of boarding and debarking, and later in the program the students will be responsible for the upkeep and maintenance of the craft as they get them underway. Intense cross-training is required in case a specialist is injured in combat. Time management accountability and responsibility are stressed during SWCC school. For many SWCC students this is their first experience where being on time and in the right place is crucial to the overall outcome of the mission, and lives may someday be depending in their punctuality, and preciseness.

At the conclusion of this school, students can be expected to be able to perform the following tasks:
• Describe the characteristics and capability of each Special Warfare craft
• Match, from a list, helm unit controls and indicators to their functional descriptions
• Given diagrams of basic hydraulic steering/propulsion/transmission systems and a list of corresponding component technology, label the diagrams with correct terminology
• Operate the emergency steering system of a Special Warfare craft
• Operate a variety of transceivers (both secure and non-secure), radios, radars, and the corresponding terminology
• Disassemble, clean, and assemble a variety of light weapons, including the craft machine gun, M-14 and M-16 rifles, and .50 caliber heavy machine gun
• Proficiency in the use of larger weapons systems such as the Mk.19 grenade launcher, 60mm mortar and 20mm-25mm machine guns
• Become proficient in the use of night vision goggles, hand grenades, and various pyrotechnics (including flares, smoke grenades, and hand-help pop flares)

The final stage of SWCC teaches the advanced skills required of a Navy Special Warfare crewman. These include a demonstrated understanding of personal survival skills, such as operations in a variety of climates, water survival techniques, and advanced first aid. This latter course work includes treatment of burns, CPR certification (to American Red Cross standards) and transport of an injured victim. Other course work is geared towards an overall understanding of special operations and low intensity conflict. As a crewman may be expected to operate

SBU-20, RIB detachment on board the USS Trenton, off the coast of Sardinia, preparing the RIB's for joint operations and training with the Spanish and Italian naval special warfare forces. (U.S. Navy)

SBU-13, RIB detachment boats, on the deck of the USS Ogden, in the port of Hong Kong. (SBU-13 was decommissioned several years ago). (U.S. Navy)

SBU-13, RIB detachment conducting training operations in the port of Bahrain. (U.S. Navy)

SBU-13 RIB detachment exercising the 24' RIB, in a slightly tight turn. (U.S. Navy)

anywhere in the world, he must also be proficient in navigation by map and electronic means (LORAN, GPS NAVSTAR, etc.), as well as international "Rules of the Road". The Rules include travel in international waters, buoy recognition, underway safety guidelines, and transiting inland waterways.

Sailors may not volunteer for a spot in a Special Boat Unit until the three-year point in a four-year sea-tour. Acceptance requires approval of a professional development review board as well as the applicant's commanding officer. Though specific shore tour lengths have yet to be established, he'll rotate between sea and shore duty within the community. A select number of these specialists will be allowed to remain in this community for their entire careers, or as long as they want to stay, as is the case with SEALs and other special warriors. In 1997, there were more than 600 billets available to third and second class petty officers. These volunteer positions are all-male as current U.S. policy forbid females from ground combat jobs. Entry into the community is open to enlisted men in most ratings. But sailors in deck and engineering ratings have the best chance of succeeding in the unit.

Recent Operations and Exercises

The Special Boat Units have deployed on an increasingly wide variety and number of international operations and exercises. "Baltops

94" was conducted in conjunction with the Polish Navy and its special forces assets. U.S. participation included SBU-20 Detachment-Delta, SEAL Team TWO-Delta Platoon, and Explosive Ordnance Disposal Detachment-Sigonella. Highlighting the exercise was an at-sea static-line parachute drop followed by recovery from Polish naval vessels.

A Special Boat Units detachment worked in conjunction with the *USS Independence* carrier battle group in "Exercise Tandem Thrust 97," from March 10-22. Special operations forces, including U.S. Navy SEAL and EOD personnel and Australian Clearance Diving Team elements, also took part in this exercise conducted with the Australian Defense Forces. This large operation involved more than 26,500 personnel and 43 vessels from both nations. The SBU detachment

SBU-13, RIB detachment taking the opportunity to check out all operational equipment and gear prior to sailing for Saudi Arabia and Kuwait. (U.S. Navy)

SBU-13 RIBs, with the second RIB almost concealed behind the wake. It is extremely important that the Combatant Craft Crewmen can operate their assigned craft in all sea states and conditions, at the same time maintaining control at all times. (U.S. Navy)

supported amphibious operations conducted on Townshend Island and Sabina Point.

SBU also conducts a regular program of training special boat units from other nations. Of course, the units involved often share a dual role, both training and supporting ongoing U.S. military operations. For example, in 1995, a detachment from SBU-20 embarked aboard *USS Ponce* (LPD-15) are on short notice standby for tasking in support of contingencies associated with United Nations peacekeeping efforts in Bosnia-Herzegovina. A primary focus was search and rescue, supporting the helicopters of the regular Navy. The SBU crew-members recently took part in "Exercise African Eagle," an amphibious exercise with the Royal Moroccan Navy and Naval Infantry. During the exercise SBU-20, Detachment-India, had great success in supporting the SEALs' training

Panama. SBU-26, conducting training exercises. (U.S. Navy)

A RIB is underway for training and exercises with SEAL members. (U.S. Navy)

of the Moroccan combat swimmers. This training took place during the course of the detachment's six month deployment as part of the Mediterranean Amphibious Ready Group.

Reserves

Naval Special Warfare forces provide covert operation and special mission capabilities to the nation's sea services and joint commands. Special Warfare fully integrates Reserve personnel into global administrative, operational, and combat requirements. The nearly 1,400 members of the Sea-Air-Land force (SEALs), combatant craft crew members, and support technicians of the Naval Special Warfare Reserve Component provide the continuous logistical support for Active-duty SEAL Teams and Special Boat Units (SBUs). SBU Reserve personnel man two of the Navy's three riverine SBUs, operating all riverine craft on the same basis as their Active-duty peers. Other SBU combatant craft crew members augment each of the two "coastal" SBUs.

Naval Special Warfare Reserve personnel provide extensive peacetime support to their gaining commands on a daily basis. They also expand personnel resources to meet unique joint operating requirements such as those for Joint Special Operations Task Forces (JSOTFs) worldwide. Indeed, from January to July 1995, the commander of JSOTF ONE - part of Operation Joint Endeavor in the former Yugoslavia - was a Selected Reserve SEAL officer.

Recently, the Reserves have undergone a minor reorganization. SBU-11 was decommissioned on September 6, 1997, on Mare Island near San Francisco. A number of it's personnel went selected for transfer to the Sacramento Navy Reserve detachment, with most of the unit's craft sent to SBU-22 in New Orleans. In a final demonstration of SBU capabilities, SBU-11 conducted a joint "mission" with U.S. Army Rangers using four Boston Whalers in a nighttime demonstration. SBU-11 deployed to the Persian Gulf in 1988 and most recently aided in the rescues of civilians from nearby townships during a series of floods.

Another major reserve unit is SBU-22 which comprises nearly half of the U.S. Navy's riverine capability along with SBU-11 in San Diego, CA. This unit is made up of 120 reservists and 100 active-duty personnel. Elements of SBU-22 were among the first units deployed to the Persian Gulf for Operations Desert Shield/Storm, arriving just two days after the Iraqi Army crossed into Kuwait. SBU-22 regularly deploys to Central America for training and exercises. A detachment from this unit was deployed to Namibia in 1995 to teach that nation's patrol boat fleet in counter-narcotics operations.

New Arrivals

The most recent arrival to the SBUs has been the Mk.V Special Operations Craft (SOC). The Mk.V is used, like many traditional SBU craft, to carry Special Operations Forces (SOF), primarily SEALs, into and out of operations where the threat to these forces is considered to be low to medium. They also support limited coastal patrol and interruption of enemy activities. According to official U.S. Navy information, Mk.Vs are organized into detachments comprised of two boats, crews and a

PBL, conducting training. Preparing to insert U.S. Navy SEALs. (U.S. Navy)

deployment support package mounted on cargo transports. The detachment can be delivered in-theater rapidly by two C-5 Galaxy aircraft, by a well or flight deck equipped surface ships and, if appropriate, under their own power. The detachment can be deployable within forty-eight hours of notification and ready for operations within twenty-four hours of arrival at a forward operating base. They can operate from shore facilities, from well-deck equipped ships or from ships with appropriate crane and deck space capabilities.

A footnote to the SOC Mk.V must be the new Cyclone-class Patrol Boats. These 170-foot vessels are often erroneously attributed to the Special Boat Units. This is not the case as while the PC's are indeed deployed with NSW, they are manned by regular Navy crews, not SBU personnel. It bears mentioning that no small number of complaints from within the Naval Special Warfare establishment have been raised against the introduction of this new class into the NSW fleet, primarily from SEAL operators. It has been argued that the ships were designed by those not intimately familiar with the requirements of special warfare. They have voiced concerns that the new ships are undergunned with two 25mm Mk.38 machine guns, two .50 caliber machine guns, two Mk.19 automatic grenade launchers, and six Stinger missiles for defense from enemy aircraft. Another complaint is that they are impractical in their design, as they are able to carry only eight SEALs (as many as the much smaller and cheaper Mk.V), while requiring a crew of four officers and twenty-four enlisted personnel (only one of which is NSW/SWCC-qualified). To date, the Navy has taken delivery of thirteen patrol crafts, produced by Bollinger Shipyards in New Orleans, Louisiana, with nine operating out of the Naval Amphibious Base, Little Creek, Va., and four home-ported at the Naval Amphibious Base, Coronado, California. The primary mission of these ships is coastal patrol and interdiction surveillance.

Organization

The Special Boat Squadrons are organized along the following lines:

Special Boat Sqn. 1 – SBS-1: Coronado, CA
Special Boat Unit 11[*]– SBU-11 Vallejo, CA
Special Boat Unit 12 – SBU-12 Coronado, CA

Special Boat Sqn. 2 – SBS-2 : Little Creek, VA
Special Boat Unit 20 – SBU-20 Little Creek, VA
Special Boat Unit 22 (NR) – SBU-22 New Orleans, LA
Special Boat Unit 26 – SBU-26 Naval Station Rodman, Panama
*recently decommissioned

SBU Craft

U.S. naval craft types currently in the U.S. Navy Special Boat Unit inventory:

Type: **Patrol Boat, River (PBR)**
Primary Mission: River and Tideway Patrols
Length: 31 ft. 11 in.
Crew: Four
Weapons: Two machine gun mounts (one forward, one aft)
  Two .50 caliber machine guns

An SBU PBR (Patrol Boat, River) which was the same type that Medal of Honor recipient E.J. Williams saw action with in Vietnam. (U.S. Navy)

Mk.V, on its trailer with the tractor ready to tow. This Mk.V was on its trailer, for all to see, at the recent SBU-20 Building Dedication. (U.S. Navy)

PBR, with ballistic plating shields and numerous weapons on board, this is an extremely effective close quarters Riverine Combatant Craft. From the Vietnam veterans who fought from her decks to today's sailors, in Central and South America, who still man them, this is their favorite. (U.S. Navy)

	Capable of mounting 7.62mm, 20mm machine guns, or 40mm grenade launcher
	Small arms
Notes:	This craft saw widespread deployment during the Vietnam War.

Type:	**Patrol Boat, Light (PBL)**
Primary Mission:	River and tideway patrols
Length:	24 ft. and 28 ft. Boston Whalers
Crew:	Two to four, depending on mission
Weapons:	Varied; M-60 or .50 caliber machine guns, or small arms.

Type:	**24-foot Rigid Inflatable Boat (RIB)**
Primary Mission:	Insertion and extraction of special forces
Length:	24 ft.
Crew:	3
Weapons:	All crew members equipped with small arms
Notes:	Saw extensive use during Operations Desert Shield/Storm

Type:	**30-foot Rigid Inflatable Boat (RIB)**
Primary Mission:	Insertion and extraction of special forces
Length:	30 ft.
Crew:	Three to five depending on mission
Weapons:	Mk.19 grenade launcher and M-60 machine gun

Notes:	Designed as a replacement for the Seafox. In widespread use throughout the U.S. special operations community.

Type:	**NSW 10-meter Rigid Inflatable Boat (RIB)**
Primary Mission:	nsertion and extraction of special forces
Length:	10 meters (33 ft.)
Crew:	3-5, depending on mission
Weapons:	Mounted Mk.19 grenade launcher and M-60 machine guns.

Type:	**Mini-Armored Troop Carrier (MATC)**
Primary Mission:	Troop transport
Length:	36 ft.
Crew:	2 (plus 16 combat-equipped SEALs or other troops)
Weapons:	Seven (7) machine gun mounts, and can include the Mk. 19 grenade launcher, M-60 machine guns, and Mk. 4 Mortar
Notes:	MATC has been withdrawn from active service and is used only for training with SBU-22.

Type:	**Mk.V SOC (Special Operations Craft)**
Primary Mission:	Long range (*over the horizon*) Insertion and Extraction of special forces
Length:	85 ft.
Crew:	16 combat heavily-equipped operators (each with

Mk.V, with CRRC (Combat Rubber Raiding Craft) loaded on the stern and two RIBs laying off the stern. (U.S. Navy)

Two Mk.V's on an unscheduled, unplanned visit to Malaga, Spain. (U.S. Navy)

their own seat—a first in a NSW craft).

Weapons: Not yet determined, but can mount a variety of weapons, including .50 cal twin, mini guns, 25mm chain guns, and Mk.19 grenade launcher

Notes: This is the newest and most expensive of all NSW craft. Capable of speeds in excess of 50 mph and highly maneuverable.

Type: **High Speed Boat (HSB)**
Primary Mission: Long range (*over the horizon*) Insertion and Extraction of special forces
Length: Varies with model
Crew: 3-5
Weapons: .50 cal machine gun and Mk.19 grenade launcher
Notes: The HSB is currently only in use by SBU-12 and saw use during Operations Desert Shield/Storm.

Type: **Swift Patrol Boat Mk.III**
Primary Mission: Coastal patrol and interdiction
Length: 64 ft. 10-3/4 in.
Crew: 10
Weapons: Varies with mission. However there are four .50 caliber machine gun mounts and three heavy weapons rings capable of mounting; 40mm cannon, 20mm machine gun, Mk.19 grenade launcher, 60mm/81mm mortar, or 25mm chaingun.
Notes: Today, the Mk.III is deployed only in Panama, although most if not all craft are currently in mothballs and will likely be sold for scrap.

Type: **Mk.IV Sea Spectre Patrol Boat**
Primary Mission: Coastal patrol and interdiction
Length: 68 ft. 4-3/4 in.
Crew: 5-8
Weapons: Two 25mm gun systems, two Mk.19 40mm machine guns, one Mk.2 81mm mortar. One .50 caliber machine gun, one M-60 machine gun, and a wide variety of small arms
Notes: The few remaining Sea Spectres are deployed only in Panama.

Different views and angles of the SOC Mk.V. (U.S. Navy)

PC-5, USS Typhoon. Originally the "dazzle" scheme was painted on the Typhoon and Scirocco. However, during their most recent Yard Period, these PCs were re-painted "Haze Gray." (U.S. Navy)

"THE KINGFISHER"

The Israel Shipyards Ltd. "Shaldag" Patrol And Special Operations Craft

Israel's defense industry has long been admired for its ability to produce weapons and equipment that is the byproduct of years of combat experience, and suited to the needs of a particular facet of the Israel Defense Forces (IDF). In the past, Israel's "soldier friendly" weapons design philosophy has included the development and production of such varied weapons as the Uzi submachine gun, the Gabriel sea-to-sea missile, the Merkava main battle tanks, and the Galil family of assault rifles. One such weapon system designed by years of bitter combat experience and expertise is the Shaldag (Kingfisher) patrol boat and special operations craft produced by Israel Shipyards Ltd. in Haifa. The Shaldag has sparked interest far beyond the boundaries of the State of Israel—from South America to the Far East and, almost, became the U.S. Navy SEALs' SOC Mk.V.

The Shaldag, a 82-foot-long craft with a top speed in excess of 50 knots, is the brainchild of Israel Shipyards Ltd. President Rear-Admiral (Res.) Ze'ev Almog, the commander of Flotilla 13 (the IDF/Navy's naval commando force) from 1968 to 1971, and the OC IDF/Navy from 1979 to 1985. It was during his tenure with Flotilla 13 that Almog came to comprehend the integral relationship between successful naval operations, especially where small units were involved. Yet it was his tenure as commander of the IDF/Navy that sparked the thought process behind building a patrol craft like the Shaldag for service with the *Heyl Ha'Yam* (IDF/Navy). Until 1979, Palestinian terrorists operating from Lebanon had made dozens of attempts to infiltrate into Israel's precarious and lengthy shoreline frontier in order to perpetrate major attacks. Indeed, these "amphibious operations" were all spectacular and bloody—from the March 1975 attack by a Black September suicide squad against Tel Aviv in which eleven were killed, to the notorious March 1978 "Country Club Massacre" when Palestinian terrorists who landed on the coast by means of two Zodiac craft proceeded to kill thirty-five civilians and wound over seventy more on the outskirts of Tel Aviv. The closing of Israel's sea lanes to terrorist infiltration a number one priority of his tenure as OC IDF/Navy—a mission that employed the coordinated efforts of Israel's fleet of missile boats, submarines, patrol craft and naval commandos—and from 1979 to the present not a single seaborne terrorist attack has succeeded even though dozens were attempted.

Yet Israel's victory in the war against seaborne terrorism was not an end to the struggle, the IDF/Navy had to take into account the improved technological means available to terrorists operating out of Lebanon, as well as those based in Syria, Libya, and Algeria. Rear-Admiral Almog, along with his staff of operations and intelligence officers were aware of terrorist factions acquiring high-speed civilian racing boats capable of reaching speeds in excess of 40 knots. Modified correctly, these speedboats could ferry in a force of over a dozen terrorists toward a target on the Israeli shore, they could travel great distances to their targets or, as is most popular in terrorist doctrine, be deployed from a mother ship (be it a disguised merchant vessel or a warship) in international waters. The Dabur patrol craft, the mainstay coast guard vessel employed by the **Heyl Ha'Yam** has a maximum speed of less than twenty knots, and armed with "light" crew mounted weapons (20mm Oerlikon cannons and .50 caliber heavy machine guns); an improved Dabur, the Super Dvora, capable of higher speeds has also entered service, yet it is no match for chasing a speedboat. Missile boats, like the Sa'ar 4, designed for long-range over the horizon strikes, are too expensive for this type of coastal patrol. Since terrorists use civilian craft as delivery vehicles to bring them to shore, such as high speed motor boats, fishing vessels, and tug or ferry ships, it is not cost effective (on

The Shaldag—a sleek, low-silhouette fast insertion craft designed with years of naval special warfare experience. The uniquely angled hull—its low draft, allowing it to operate virtually anywhere—from lakes to rivers to the open seas.

practical and tactial levels) to have missile boats deal with intercepting a suspected target from long-ranges in international waters, deploying long range weaponry such as main armament 76mm guns, or their compliment of Gabriel or Harpoon sea-to-sea missiles. Also, it is not tactically prudent or cost-effective for the $60 million Sa'ar IV missile boat, built by Israel Shipyards Ltd., to engage small boats or rubberized inflatable craft at "eyeball-to-eyeball" ranges, nor is it operationally prudent to place a multi-million dollar ship and a crew of nearly fifty so close to potential danger; as Israel's naval commandos proved during the closing days of the 1973 Yom Kippur War, one round fired from a hand-held anti-tank rocket launcher can certainly destroy a missile boat. Patrol work requires a highly cost-effective patrol craft—a fast patrol craft that can outmaneuver, outgun and outperform the speed boats and inflatable craft that terrorists (and smugglers) have added to their arsenals.

The thought process behind building a faster patrol craft was to produce "a novel techno-operational solution for combating terrorism." The mental blue-prints for such a craft were building in Ze'ev Almog's mind for years, but directing the shipyards provided him with the opportunity to see the vision through into tangible fruition. At the shipyards, Almog enlisted a team of retired Flotilla 13 comrades and IDF/Navy technical officers to form a unique conceptual think tank to design a new generation patrol craft that would be economical taking into account the complete life-cycle of the craft and integrating the most advanced technologies available to eventually produce a high speed, rough sea, multi-purpose boat, that could operate in both blue waters and riverine areas. That boat was the Shaldag, the Kingfisher.

The Shaldag was conceived with <u>six</u> primary objectives in mind: (a) to be a high-speed, highly maneuverable craft capable of physically approaching a suspect craft to within eyesight or hailing distance, and capable of pursuing a fast craft for extended ranges; (b) to provide an extremely smooth sail, even in the

The Shaldag's low draft, allowing it to literally transport naval special warfare operators onto an enemy beach, made it, in the words of one naval commando officer, "like an armored and heavily armed Zodiac!"

The Shaldag's forward mounted 20mm Oerlikon cannon, an ideal insertion support weapon, is also ideal when faced off against speed boats used by terrorists and smugglers. The 20mm Oerlikon can be replaced by a .50 caliber heavy machine gun, as well as other mounted weaponry such as a Mk.19 40mm grenade launcher or 84mm Carl Gustav anti-tank weapon.

roughest seas, to ensure that crews did not suffer from the attritioning seasickness and fatigue caused by slamming, endured in most craft in rough sea states; (c) to produce a craft with a dry deck, so that the erosion and negative effects on a crews' behavior and alertness due to drenching is eliminated, and allowing crewmen to man mounted guns and heavy machine guns without being engulfed in the spray of the waves while the ship races at top speed; (d) a low draft and excellent maneuverability for pursuing vessels in virtually all locations; (e) the capability to carry massive firepower and ample supplies of ammunition; and, (f) spaciousness, and convenient access to all operating systems.

The Shaldag's high speed is the result of the combination of a water jet propulsion system consisting of two Deutz-MWM TBD 604 B V16 water cooled marine diesel engines rated at 2,500 HP at 1,800 rpm, and the unique hull form. Two Riva-Lips steerable water jets are mounted on the transom with internal access for support and maintenance. The smooth sail and minimal slamming high speeds in rough sea states is achieved by a unique deep-V planning hull form with two risers and a novel hard chine. The Shaldag does not punch its way across high waves, but rather slices through them like, according to one of the Shaldag's designers, "a knife through butter"—even at speeds in excess of 50 knots. Up to sea states three and four, the Shaldag can maintain an average speed of 45 knots, and run fully loaded (56 tons) for 890 miles. Special wave deflectors at the bottom of the hull, two risers and novel hard chine, ensure both the upper and main decks of the Shaldag remain absolutely dry in all operating conditions. The Shaldag's design also made provisions for carrying a full compliment of weaponry, including: foredeck and aftdeck rings for 20mm Oerlikon single gun mounts; spigots for .50 caliber machine guns on both sides of the main deck and spigots for 7.62mm light machine guns. Perhaps more significantly, the Shaldag is designed to carry the most advanced weapons systems available: the foredeck is designed to carry a rapid-fire 25mm Sea-Vulcan gun, as well as various types of compact anti-tank and anti-aircraft missile systems, such as the "Nimrod" and the "Stinger." The Shaldag's designer took it into account that different operational objectives required different variations, and as a result the Shaldag's unique platform can incorparate a wide array of combination of propulsion and weapon systems while still not altering the boat's overall performance.

The ability of the Shaldag to intercept high-speed craft, and to allow the crew the opportunity to out-maneuver any opposing craft grabbed the interest of foreign powers, such as several South American and Asian powers. It was, however, the United States that provided the Kingfisher with its greatest potential. Among the first to display serious interest was the United States Coast Guard, the eleventh largest navy in the world, who considered the Shaldag as a practical and inexpensive answer to

the difficulties of intercepting drug smuggling, but the most serious customer appeared to be the U.S. Navy SEALs. The U.S. Naval Special Warfare Command displayed serious interest in the Shaldag just as the United States Special Operations Command (USSOCOM) was involved. Congressional guidelines allowed USSOCOM to unilaterally initiate the purchase of a SEALs insertion and extraction craft with four primary operational criteria: a ship capable of inserting and extracting *a platoon-size force of SEALs*; a boat that can achieve this transport task at high speed and in bring in the SEALs in *top physical condition*; a boat that is *Lockheed C-5A Galaxy transportable*; and, a craft with an acceptable price tag, as USSOCOM was directed by Congress to purchase as many as twenty or thirty such craft. The Shaldag met all of Congress' and, initially, USSOCOM's requirements, and tentative American interest in the craft soon became a full-fledged commitment to evaluate and examine the vessel. Even though it was built as a patrol craft designed for interdiction, the SEALs were impressed by the fact that a transformation into a special operations craft would require a minimum of inexpensive modifications; more importantly, perhaps, a prototype of the Shaldag <u>already existed</u> (another congressional requirement), ready for any trial and tests that would be put to it.

In October 1990, as much of the American special warfare community was preparing for action in the Persian Gulf, Rear-Admiral George Worthington, Commander, Naval Special Warfare Command, led a team of naval architects, technicians, and experienced Naval Special Warfare operators to Haifa to evaluate the Shaldag for a week of sea trials; Worthington's team returned to Haifa in January 1991 for additional rough sea trials. Although keeping their conclusions "close to the vest," the SEAL contingent was impressed by the Shaldag's speed and maneuverability; the water jet propulsion system and its rudder-system steering tool allows the Shaldag to make a full circle at 48 knots with a diameter of less that 100 meters. Not only did this feature enable the Shaldag to perform sharp, high-speed escape and evasion maneuvers if under fire, but the Shaldag does not have to slow down considerably when entering such facilities as enemy harbors for attack, or shore areas covered with tangles, growth or natural hiding places should the situation call for evasion from pursuing enemy ships. More impressively, the Shaldag can literally "stop on a dime"—its water jet propulsion allows it to go from a full 50 knots to a standstill position in eleven seconds!

According to one SEAL Special Boat Unit officer, "The Shaldag is a special operations craft with remarkable capabilities and potential." According to one of the primary USSOCOM requirements in procuring an insertion and extraction craft for the U.S. Navy SEALs was its ability to bring in a "platoon" size of men to its target in a maximum physical state at the highest possible speed. Getting the operators to their objective was only half the equation—getting them there in perfect physical condition was equally as important. "While speedboats are capable of speeds in excess of seventy and eighty knots," adds Michael Abraham, a former Flotilla 13 technical officer, an MIT graduate and one of the Shaldag's chief designers, "those speeds results in such heavy slamming, even in calm seas, that the human cargo carried is physically incapacitated for several hours after reaching land; among the ailments are seasickness, dizziness, the urinating of blood, and even more serious injuries. While the Shaldag can not travel faster than 50 plus knots, it can maintain a smooth and highly comfortable ride even in the highest state of sea unrest. This is not only important for the force of SEAL Team members in full battle gear who must assault a fortified target once the shoreline is reached, but is equally as important a factor for the highly delicate equipment carried by special operations forces into battle. Slamming and the harsh ride takes an enormous toll on this sensitive equipment—often leaving them inoperable in the field when the unit is in no position to make repairs, or perform <u>without</u> those invaluable tools is operationally foolish.

Special Boat Unit officers who tested the Shaldag in the winter of 1991 were also highly impressed with the craft's minimal draft, only 1.15 meters, which allows the vessel to operate in extremely shallow waters. In fact, this low draft allows the ship to act as a "heavily armed Zodiac craft"—the Shaldag can ferry its compliment of commandos to the edge of the shoreline, allowing them to jump off the boat and spring into immediate action, while all the time being covered by the Shaldag's weaponry.

Special operations characteristics were evident in virtually every aspect of the Shaldag's design. The Special Boat Unit officers, always concerned about the covert nature of their work and the ability to enter a target undetected, were also impressed by the Shaldag's small radar signature—due to the almost non-existent watermark produced by the propulsion system, and the unique, deflective design, of its cabin area. The Shaldag, even though a small craft designed to out-maneuver and out-race any hostile intentions, is also a sturdy vessel capable of taking fire. The hull is made of marine aluminum, with the fuel tanks located in the double bottom for safety below sea level and to minimize damage in case of being hit by enemy fire. The Shaldag, in true Israeli fashion, is also "maintenance friendly." The quality of the two MWM 604B series diesel engines together with the Riva-Lips Water Jet IRC 64DXL, Salzgitter Electronic Control System and the German REINJES gear are such that the Shaldag can endure 30,000 working hours at sea until its first overhaul. Should the ship take fire and require maintenance, the Shaldag's aftdeck is designed in such a manner that its twin engines, positioned below, can be removed and replaced in a remarkable two hours!

There were other, user friendly, aspects of the Shaldag that endeared it in the minds of the SEAL officers. Positioned above the water jets is a multi-purpose protective structure serving as an anchor for a rubber dinghy. A ladder on the platform side of the multi-purpose structure facilitates easy access to the sea for divers allowing access from the water without fear of being hit by the propellers as a result of the waterjets. Comfortable accommodations and galleys are located behind the cockpit, allowing the crew and serving personnel to reach their firing positions and battle stations without interfering with the command and control of the ship; wide passages on the decks allows the crew to pass toward their battle stations even if deck mounted guns are manned.

After reading through the SEAL Special Boat Unit report which, among other qualities, praised the Shaldag as the best solution to Naval Special Warfare needs, USSOCOM Commander-in-Chief General Carl W. Stiner wrote to Senator Robert C. Byrd, Chairman of the Senate Appropriations Committee, and praised the craft and virtually requested its acquisition. The Shaldag met all of the congressional requirements as set forth by their agreement to fund USSOCOM's procurement project. House and Senate appropriation committees stipulated that the Mk.V craft be capable of performing counter-drug and SEAL insertion and interdiction mission on rough seas. They stipulated that the craft have a range greater than 600 nautical miles sustained, and a top

speed in excess of 40 knots, and is to be armed with light caliber weapons as well as capable of firing surface-to-surface or surface-to-air missiles. The most pressing congressional demand in this age of defense procurement frugality was that USSOCOM purchase an "off-the-shelf," multi-mission boat requiring little or no development cash.

On August 6, 1993, the United States Special Operations Command (USSOCOM) awarded the SOC Mk.V prototype contracts to Halter Marine (two prototypes) and Peterson builders. The Shaldag design, which had been proposed to USSOCOM by Swift Ships, was found technically acceptable and operationally sufficient, the Shaldag did not receive an award, even though NAVSOC commander Admiral George Worthington and his team had tested the Shaldag, in both calm seas and stormy waters, and had, through CINCSOCOM General Stiner, reported that, "There is no comparable craft to the Shaldag."

The SEALs, especially in this less stable and unpredictable world, are going to be more of a covert naval special warfare force than ever before—even more than during the Cold War. From Somalia to Bosnia, from South America to the Persian Gulf and the Middle East, the new world order presents an endless listing of trouble spots that will require the deployment of the SEALs in top-secret covert assignments: from intelligence-gathering to sabotage, infiltration and extraction to raiding. These missions will demand that the SEALs deploy with speed, stealth, and tactical surprise. Perhaps the Shaldag will be one such means for their delivery into harms way.

Whether it will be patrolling Israel's precarious shoreline against Palestinian terrorist squads, or ferrying U.S. Navy SEALs to and from their covert objectives, the Shaldag's unique "technological design" promises to be the standard that all vessels of its type will be measured against for a good many years to come.

The Shaldag - Main Data	
Length, Overall-	4.80 Meters
Beam, Overall-	6.00 Meters
Draft -	1.15 Meters
Standard Displacement -	50 tons
Full Displacement -	56 tons/62 tons
Speed -	50 knots plus
Range: at 45k -	890 N. Miles
Range: at 33kn -	990 N. Miles
Endurance -	48-72 Hours (depending on speed and operational profile)
Crew -	8

A landing dock, situated right above the water-jet propulsion system, allows for a safe-docking of a Zodiac craft, even when both rubber inflatable and "mother ship" are traveling at high-speeds.

LEGIONNAIRES IN THE JUNGLE

Yves Debay

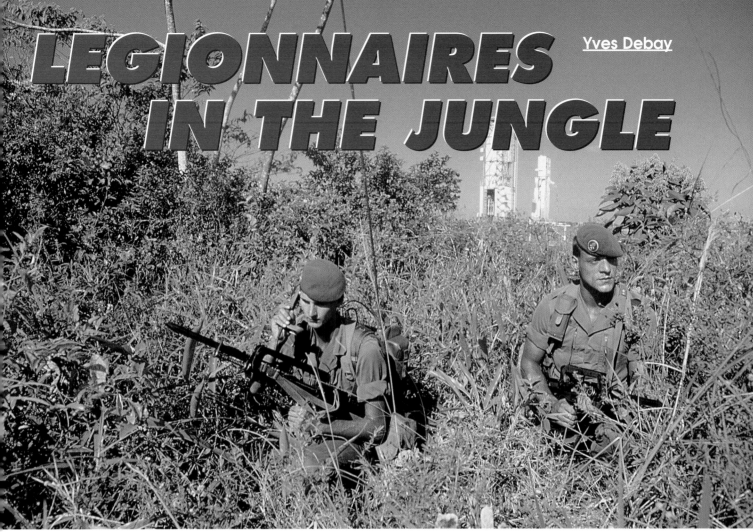

The main mission of the 3ème REI is to assume the security of the CGS which is the main space center well placed near the equator. Here legionnaires on guard before a launch.

A Legionnaire on guard duty in the perimeter of the CGS (Centre Spatial Guyanais).

In the world of military elite units, there is usually the "legend," the myth and the bravado, and then there is the "reality" of a unit's true capabilities. Yet in the case of the French Foreign Legion, perhaps the most endeared and romantic of the world's elite military formations, legend and reality are one in the same. The Foreign Legion's *3ème Régiment Etranger d'Infanterie* (3rd Foreign Legion Infantry Regiment) is the personification of such a force—one where the harsh training of its men and exotic locations of its deployments blend to produce one of the most remarkable and durable military units in service anywhere in the world today. And, nowhere is the Hollywood-version of what it's like to serve in the Legion more accurate than with the 3rd Foreign Legion Infantry Regiment during a deployment and training stint in Guyana where, in the backdrop of the equatorial forest, a soldier must not only be able to survive with a rifle slung over his shoulder and a rucksack tearing into his back, but be able to contend with jaguars and anacondas that can lurk behind every bend and up every tree.

The 3ème REI, under the command of the Colonel Lalanne Berdouticq is, today, the most decorated regiment of the French Foreign Legion. The sole French force in the West Indies and Guyana, the regiment consists of thirty-eight officers, 116 NCOs and 583 legionnaires. Remarkably, more than fifty nationalities are represented in the ranks of the regiment—over 60% of which are non-French-speaking. The average of age the legionnaires in the unit is twenty-five-years-old, though most are experienced veterans of unquestioned military skill and unflinching valor.

Valor, in fact, has been the call to arms of the Foreign Legion's most decorated regiment for nearly a century. The 3éme REI is the heir of the RMLE formed on November 15, 1915, which consolidated the survivors of the 1st and 2éme decimated after the first year of World War One and,

The Swedish-built Hägglunds BV-206 all-terrain tracked vehicle—the ideal means of transport in marsh-lands with swamps surrounding the CGS.

The BV-206 consists of two units linked together with a steering unit. It is fully amphibious being propelled in the water by its tracks.

A legionnaire of Norwegian origin is taking cover among the jungle vegetation. The regiment has over fifty different nationalities represented in its ranks.

Patrols along jungles routes where one never knows who or what may be encountered.

as part of the Moroccan division to which it belongs, the RMLE participated in many of the great battle on the Western Front, such as: Belloy en Santerre, Auberive, Cumieres, Le bois de Hangard, and la montagne de Paris. On September 14, 1918, the RMLE pierced the once-thought-of-as-unpassable Hindenburg-Line, a date celebrated by the unit in the *Feast of the Fourragére*. Sixty-six officers, 208 NCOs and 1,891 legionaries were killed during World War One, following which the regiment returned to Morocco where it became the 3éme REI. During the Second World War, in 1942, 3éme fought Rommel's Afrika Korps in the marshes of Zaghoan, and in 1944 it battled the Germans hard in the campaigns of Alsace and Colmar. A year after crossing the Rhine and pushing into Austria, 3éme REI found itself en route to another hot spot of bloody distinction—Indochina. 3éme REI was the lead unit in the ferocious battle of Colonial Road 4 (RC4) and Dien Bien Phu. The TOE (*Territoires d' Outre-Mer, Overseas Territory*) was awarded after the regiment lost seventy-seven officers, 364 NCOs, and 3,396 legionnaires—a casualty rate that dwarfed the carnage suffered by the regiment during the First World War. From Indochina, the regiment found itself under fire once again in Algeria where, along the lines of its proud heritage, the force distinguished itself for heroism.

On-call deployments are a Foreign Legion specialty—after all, nothing can personify the Legion's traditional mission of trekking to the most remote and most inhospitable stretches of the planet to serve French interests. But on Guyana, where the unit is known as "Guardians of Space," 3éme REI has assumed a new and all-important function—serving as the protector for France's *Centre Spatial Guyannaíre* (CGS)—the Guyanese Space Center. While protection of the interior perimeter is the responsibility of the French Gendarmerie (Police), defense of the external perimeter and surrounding areas is reserved solely to the Legion.

The only way to be resupplied for the deep jungle patrols is the helicopters. The landing zone is created by one of the most effective means of clearing a jungle stretch-with explosive.

Lunch of the day—Guyanese style!

A trained sharpshooter with a rifle like the FR-F2 and a good IL scope can slow down entire enemy columns along jungle roads.

A motorized canoe remains the best way to move across the Guyanese jungle to conduct military operations—here men of the 2nd Company on patrol.

Legionnaires on alert, with weapons facing outwards as the canoe speeds through the Guyanese river.

Legionnaires are trained to fire their FAMAS assault rifles from a moving canoe with pinpoint accuracy.

A speeding canoe with legionnaires of the 2nd Company on board on a patrol in the Guyanese rivers.

During rocket launches, legionnaries mount aggressive—and heavily armed—patrols in the vast stretches of marsh and jungle that surrounds the CGS.

The importance of the CGS to French defense interests is all-encompassing, and the security responsibilities reserved for 3éme REI is enormous. The unit trains year-round to respond to terrorist attacks and hostage-taking incidents, as well as hit-and-run attacks by guerrilla forces. The fact that 3éme REI trains regularly is nothing extraordinary—after all, being prepared for battle is part of the Legion's proud heritage. But the fact that they are strategically situated in a part of the West Indies that although quiet, has the potential for low-intensity conflict, makes them one of the premier rapid deployment forces in the area—a fact not lost to both American and British commanders maintaining military forces in the area. 3éme REI—"Detachment Jaguar" is a permanent operational force of 500 men that is on-call, twenty-four-hours-a-day to respond anywhere and everywhere in the region by means of armored transport, ship or helicopter.

Like both the U.S. Marine Corps and the U.S. Army's 75th Ranger Regiment (Airborne), 3ème REI specializes in seizing beachheads and taking over airfields. The unit routinely trains in seizing—and controlling—small cities as well as maintaining order and control in the towns they capture; the unit's regimen of close-quarter urban combat training, considered among the finest in the world, focuses on speed and pinpoint accuracy, rather than relaying on massive firepower.

In the jungle, however, and in the rain forests, there are few units as skilled as experienced as 3éme REI—they can ford rivers without any difficulty, they can survive i the field for weeks relying on local water supplies and the local shrubbery and wildlife for sustenance. As much of the unit's responsibilities border around the Brazilian border, 3éme REI conducts numerous "deep penetration missions in the jungle."

To ensure its ability to execute its diverse and many military missions, 3éme REI maintains a *Compagnie de Comandement et Soutien*, better known by its acronym of CCS for Command and Support Company, a CEA (*Compagnie d'Eclairage et d'Appui*, for Reconnaissance and Weapon Company) and 2ème and 3ème combat companies. Other Foreign Legion units are routinely rotated to serve with 3ème REI for advanced jungle training and the Legion's jungle-warfare center, known as CEFE, is renown throughout the world

Created in 1974, the CEFE is, according to its commanding officer (the legendary Captain Herique), "More a specialized survival school than a commando training center." CEFE's three primary missions include: to prepare units to confront difficulties of the combat in a rain forest; to reflect to the various techniques of combat in jungle; to strengthen military and technical knowledge as well as the cohesion of units as a result of their arduous stay in the wilds of nature. Officer candidates in the French military are routinely passed through CEFE, as are units from Allied armies, such as U.S. Marines, Canadian special forces, and Venezuelan commandos, as well as other French combat units stationed in the "Zone West Indies—Guyana." Of the instruction offered at the jungle combat center, "survival and trap making" is of particular interest. Jungle warfare students learn, for example, how to make a "péconia," a circular hoist made of crooked supple branches that allow a soldier to climb up trees and seek tropical fruit. "Narcisse," an indigenous Indian who know the jungle perfectly, gives courses on plants and edible berries, and how to catch fish using nothing but improvised tools.

Military operations in the jungle are very difficult—the jungle can be both incredibly beautiful and deceptive in its dangers and the terrain inhibits and camouflages. According to Legionnaire Janssen, a native of

A Legionnaire takes aim with his FAMAS assault rifle, looking for potential threats from the jungle.

Far from France, an NCO ponders deep in thought while on patrol on this Guyanese river.

Norway, jungle operations are the measure of one's worth as a soldier and as a member of the Foreign Legion. "The deep penetration patrol in the jungle constitute an unforgettable reward once over, but it is a very trying experience. Recently, we had to evacuate a legionnaire hit hard by malaria. We had to carry our wounded comrade off by stretcher over an eight-kilometer long path, through uncuttable jungle, until we reached the helicopter landing zone, and evacuated the sick soldier. We were lucky. The jungle had been traversed weeks earlier before by one of our patrols. Had it been a 'virgin' stretch of the rain forest, the march would have taken us nearly a day to complete." "Legionnaire Dej," a young and very cheerful Russian-native, continues. "Operating in the jungle is hard, very hard, but at the same time very interesting. While we cross the jungle with the forty-five kilograms of equipment on our back, we sometime see some large game and very large reptiles escaping us, while smaller beasts are usually indifferent to us. Carrying one's rifle through the bush, while the rains pour down incessantly, turns our uniforms into evaporating rags and our weapons into slippery rods of rust. Mosquitoes gnaw at our skin, and microorganism dig craters in our flesh. In the jungle you fight two enemies—your armed adversary and the uncontrolled anger of nature!"

Within the CCS of the 3ème REI exists a small unique unit known by the acronym GTMF (*Groupe de Transport Maritime et Fluvial* or *Maritime and River Transport Group*) that is responsible for transport

A Legionnaire, armed with a FAMAS assault rifle, is about to land from the canoe. Often the sergeant is armed with a Mossberg shotgun, such a weapon proves very efficient to improve the food in the jungle or close combat.

Legionnaires relaxing in a landing craft, enjoying the Guyanese sunshine.

Some landing crafts are used to ferry men and vehicles or heavy equipment when necessary.

Before a rocket is about to be launched at the CGS, all the combat squads go to the full alert status.

The VAB armored personnel carrier in the background is the Legionnaires battle taxi in Guyana. It can provide additional firepower if needed.

The Legionnaire on the left has taken up a position with an 89mm LRAC rocket launcher, ready to encounter any enemy armored vehicles.

A Matra Mistral SATCP low altitude surface-to-air missile system on its tripod launcher, it is one of the most sophisticated and accurate weapons of the 3ème REI, deployed for air defense at the Space Center.

and landing craft abilities on the many waterways and tributaries of the Amazon. Transport needs are enhanced by a mechanized force consisting of light-tracked vehicles Hägglunds BV-206. Their tracked-vehicle is ideal for negotiating the hostile terrain and marshy areas around the space center, as well as the other surrounding areas. The CEA (*Compagnie d'Eclairage et d'Appui*) is a support mechanized force consisting of 150 men and consists of the heavy-weapons carried by the unit, such as 20mm anti-aircraft guns, 81mm mortars and Mistral missiles.

In the world of the military elite, two kind of units operate in the jungle. Those that are defeated by the elements, and those who become one with them. 3ème REI is the kind of unit that has never allowed the elements, natural or man made, to interfere with its missions—from the killing fields of France and the rice-paddy hell of Indochina, the legionnaires of 3ème REI are rewriting the manual on military professionalism in the jungles of Guyana.

This Mistral missile team is guarding the Guyanese Space Center against intruders from the air. Once or twice a year the Mistral platoon is returned to France for live firing at the Biscarosse training range.

With a skilled pilot like Sergeant-Major Santos y Morales, the Pétrel ULM is the ideal means for air surveillance of the Space Center. Note that the plane seen here flying over the Kourou River is painted with the green and red marking of the Legion.

One of the 20mm automatic anti-aircraft guns of the CEA. Of course this weapon can also be used efficiently against ground or naval targets, as well.

The Tarasque 53T2 20mm automatic anti-aircraft gun. This is a very effective weapon with a high rate of fire. Its low weight makes it easily transportable across rough terrain. It can also be carried slung under a helicopter.

Under the careful watch of instructors, young draftees from France undergo the obstacle course of the Regina commando training center.

Learning the tricks of survival in the jungle by utilizing the indigenous plants and crafts.

In the jungle you eat what you catch—sometimes these tastes can be absolutely awful, though sometimes they can be absolutely beguiling.

A well decorated company sergeant major, such NCOs are the backbone of elite unit like the Legion.

Even in South America, the tradition of the Legion are kept like this sentry at the regiment gate dressed in full Legion regalia with white képi and épaulettes.

To live in the jungle you must get used to meeting strange and not always friendly animals like this anaconda. Some legionnaires, mainly the seasoned veteran, consider the snake to be a delicious meal.

The regimental band with all the glory and pride of the Legion, some may think it old fashioned but in the Legion where traditions still is one of the main power sources. It should be noted that the musicians are also the regiment's mortar crews.

THE ISRAEL DEFENSE FORCES AIRBORNE CORPS
Steven Harlov

The Winged Serpent is the IDF para brigade's insignia. (IDF)

Where The Bible Meets The Bullet

Over the past fifty years since the establishment of the modern State of Israel, the Israel Defense Forces airborne corps has gained a reputation as one of the finest elite fighting forces in the world. While the Israeli "*Tzanhanim*" (Hebrew for parachutists) have certainly had their share of combat successes and failures, victories and losses, this reputation has been won in large part due to the strategic audacity and global impact of their operations.

The Israel Defense Forces was mustered in as the official army of the State of Israel in 1948, developing out of the pre-independence fledgling defense organization, the Hagannah. The slaughter of Europe's Jews during the Holocaust gave impetus to the rapid development of a modern Israeli Army, and many Jews who emigrated to the new state had fought with Allied forces during World War Two, where field operations had convinced them of the need for special operations units; airborne-

qualified and capable of inflicting damage on the enemy in unequal proportion to their numbers. The very first Israeli paratroopers had already been in action during the war — European refugees who had escaped to Palestine, been parachute trained by British forces and then dropped behind Axis lines as forward observers and saboteurs. And while these brave operatives had little impact on the outcome of the war, the airborne battles at Crete, Normandy and Arnhem impressed the new Israeli IDF commanders of the need for the airborne option.

In 1956, Israeli paratroopers took their place in the annuals of world airborne history. For nearly ten years, Israel had alone repulsed the onslaughts of all of its Arab neighbors, refusing to be driven into the Mediterranean Sea. However, in that year President Nasser of Egypt took unilateral action to nationalize the Suez Canal and threatened to invade Israel once more through the Sinai Desert. Britain and France joined forces with Israel to foil Nasser's plans, and the entire IDF 202nd Parachute Battalion was dropped from C-47s into Sinai's Mitla Pass, successfully preventing an Egyptian incursion northward. The Israeli airborne corps had proved its worth, and would remain integral to all future combat operations.

By 1967, the *Tzanhanim* had developed into unquestionably the finest elite fighting force in the Middle East. It was an all volunteer outfit, attracting the very best of Israel's "*kibbutzniks*" (the young farmers from collective settlements) and those high-school graduates who thought they had the right stuff. But Israeli paratroopers were expected not to rely on air delivery, or even armored transport. Their legs would carry them over

A new class of jumpers is entertained to the do's—and don'ts of jumping at the Tel Nof training center. (Samuel Katz)

A practice run from one of the jump towers at Tel Nof. (Samuel Katz)

Paratroop trainees practice from Tel Nof's 30-foot tower. (IDF)

At the jump training base at Tel Nof, students and veterans listen in on a PLF lecture, as the mock-up fuselage of an IAF C-130 is readied for a different class. (Samuel Katz)

In June of that year, the combined armies of Syria, Jordan, Iraq and Egypt stood poised to invade the minuscule Jewish state once more, but Israeli leaders opted for a lightning preemptive air strike that destroyed the opposing air forces on the ground. Immediately thereafter, tanks rolled on all fronts, with the battlefield situation fluctuating so rapidly that the pre-planned drops of the airborne brigade were abandoned. Instead, Israeli paras were rushed to defend Jerusalem aboard tourists buses! After three days of bitter hand-to-hand combat, the *Tzanhanim* wrestled the capital from the Jordan's elite Arab Legion, and their legend grew to heroic proportions in the eyes of Israel and the world.

For a short period of time, Israel bathed in the glory of her victory, convinced that she could stand alone against any attack. However, the Arab confrontation states resorted to harassment tactics, particularly in the south, where Egyptian commandos regularly raided Israeli lines. By this time, the IDF had put a great deal of effort into developing airborne-qualified recon and commando units of its own. The Israeli navy began utilizing its super secret Naval Commandos (Flotilla 13) in bold strikes deep into Egyptian territory. The *Tzanhanim* had their own elite commando units such as *Sayeret Tzanhanim* (Para Recon), which proved itself in heliborne raids on both fronts, and *Sayeret Shaked* (Almond Recon), whose desert foxes roamed the wastes of the Negev and Sinai aboard motorcycles. But first and foremost in the special operations order of battle, was a small, airborne-qualified, recon commando unit that reported directly to General Headquarters of the IDF. It was modeled on the British SAS and called *Sayeret Mat'kal* - General Staff Recon - and due to the fact that these faceless men could be tasked directly by only the IDF's supreme commanders, they earned the appropriate nick name, "The Chief of Staff's Boys."

First time jumpers line up outside the chute shed, where they are for the first time going to suit up with their T-10s, and muster the courage to leap out of a perfectly sound aircraft 1,200 feet above the ground. The sign above the entrance to the rigger's work station reads "Just try and jump without us!" (Samuel Katz)

hundreds of kilometers, their shooting skills with the Belgian FN and Israeli made Uzi 9mm submachine gun honed in endless training exercises. Officers never remained in the rear while their troops fought it out up front. The Paratrooper's motto was, "Follow Me!," and of course the unit had the highest officer and NCO casualty rate of any modern combat outfit. The coveted red beret was awarded only to those men who had completed the grueling "*maslool*," a stint of basic training unequaled by any other IDF outfit for length and hardship, and you could easily identify a *Tzanhan* by the French "lizard" camouflage uniform issued only to the elite.

Jump-masters gauge the wind during a late afternoon jump. (Samuel Katz)

"Just in case," IDF ambulances stand at the ready to deal with any jump injuries. (Samuel Katz)

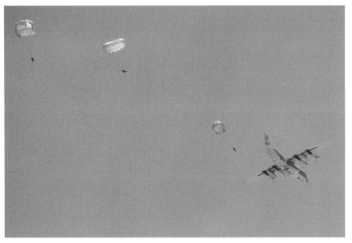

Nothing is as peaceful as the glide to the Palmachim LZ from 1,200 feet. (Samuel Katz)

As the long line of static line jumpers moves in to the parade area, free-fallers and the square rigs glide gently to earth. (Samuel Katz)

If only the best volunteered for the paratroops, then the boys who volunteered for *Sayeret Mat'kal* were the cream of the volunteer crop. They were the brightest of their schools, the most die-hard athletes, their family lineage had to pass rigorous security checks. If they survived the first months of their training, their reward was anonymity, as they claimed to be serving as nothing more than "simple paratroopers," while wearing uniforms and ranks that upheld the lie. The name of their outfit was never mentioned in the press and their most successful missions did not make the evening news. *Sayeret Mat'kal* snatched Syrian generals from their staff car convoys, blew up Egyptian command centers and "liberated" Russian radar equipment. And at last, when the Arab armies turned to terrorists to conduct their struggle by proxy, *Sayeret Mat'kal* was the answer.

After the Six-Day-War, while a War of Attrition raged on the Golan Heights and in the Sinai Desert, *Mat'kal* waged a war of anti-terrorism against Palestinian air hijackers and the sea-borne guerrillas who invaded the Israeli coast to slaughter civilians in frontier Kibbutz and Moshav agricultural settlements, hotels and nursery schools. When a Sabena airliner was hijacked and landed in Tel Aviv, *Mat'kal* operators — dressed as aircraft mechanics in white coveralls — liberated the passengers and killed the hijackers. When Palestinian terrorists assaulted the beaches of Tel Aviv and took over the Savoy Hotel, *Sayeret Mat'kal* took the building down and the terrorists out. As always, they executed their missions with ferocity and split-second timing, then disappeared back into the shadows. By this time, you could not volunteer for *Sayeret Mat'kal*. If you were lucky, you might be invited to test for this most elite of all the airborne special operations outfits.

An IDF para jump-master rallies his first-time jumpers in line following their virgin leap from 1,200 feet. (Samuel Katz)

Paratroopers ready an M113 for an aerial drop during exercises in the Negev. (IDF Spokesman)

IDF "stretcher marches" are long, painful, and the "backbone" exercise of the para brigade. (IDF Spokesman)

Foreign paratroopers are annually invited to jump with the Tzanhanim. Seen here, an American visitor awaits the arrival of an IAF C-130.

In October of 1973, the State of Israel nearly lost its life. The problem was an arrogant refusal to read the warning signs correctly — that the combined forces of Syria and Egypt were about to launch a massive invasion on Yom Kippur, the holiest of all Israeli holidays. Once again, rapid and critical battlefield developments made an airborne drop out of the question, especially since Israel's enemies were now equipped with swarms of Russian SAMs that were bringing down Israel Air Force Phantom F-4s and Skyhawks by the dozens. The newly acquired Hercules C-130s in use by the paratroopers would have been quick fodder for the SAM umbrellas.

Instead, the *Tzanhanim* once more arrived on the battlefield via soft wheels and armored personnel carriers. In the city of Suez, they paid heavily in ferocious house-to-house combat. In Sinai, their battle for the Chinese Farm cost them an entire generation of young volunteers. On the Golan Heights, their support with a large heliborne raid proved critical in recapturing Mount Hermon — the Israeli observation post that is called "The Eyes of Israel." No one could deny that the *Tzanhanim* had once more fought valiantly for their country and reputation, but for awhile they would retire to lick their wounds.

In July of 1976, Israeli airborne troops were the point men for perhaps the most famous long-range rescue mission in modern history. Palestinian and German terrorists hijacked an Air France air bus en route

During a visiting jump by international paratroopers, the true backbone of the IDF Airborne Corps, its women, displays the arduous and delicate task of readying chutes for jumps. (Samuel Katz)

Although the pressure is enormous and the responsibility in their work is truly a matter of life-and-death, the camaraderie and back-breaking work among the riggers, all of whom are girls eighteen-to-twenty years of age, is truly inspiring. (Samuel Katz)

This Israeli paratrooper medic (identified by the triangle flash on the back of his helmet) is also an expert with the FN MAG 7.62mm light machine-gun.

to Tel Aviv, with half it's passengers being Israeli citizens. The terrorists flew the plane to Uganda, where the mad dictator Idi Amin welcomed them with open arms, even as they released all but the Jewish passengers and threatened to execute them all if a series of absurd demands were not met. While the Israeli cabinet pretended to acquiesce to the demands, a combined rescue force of IDF airborne troops, including *Sayeret Mat'kal*, Para Recon and Golani Recon (the reconnaissance force of the 1st Golani Infantry Brigade) trained round the clock for the raid. On the evening of July 4, as Americans celebrated their bicentennial, the Israeli C-130s flew non-stop from Tel Aviv to Entebbe Airport in Uganda, eliminated all of the terrorists, freed the hostages and spirited them back to Israel by air. It was a special operations masterstroke that has not yet been equaled by any nation.

In 1982, the *Tzanhanim* were once more the spearhead of a military assault. This time it was a bid to drive a Palestinian terrorist "mini-state" from Lebanon. *Tzanhanim* landed by sea, by helicopter and aboard APCs, then spearheaded the Israeli drive for Beirut, engaging in vicious hand-to-hand and house-to-house battles with every elite Palestinian terrorist faction that had a foothold in Lebanon, as well as Syrian infantry, armor and airborne units of high caliber. While the war itself became a hotly contested issue in the Israeli cabinet and among the populace, the performance of Israel's ever-faithful *Tzanhanim* could not be questioned.

Today, the intensive training of Israel's Airborne still follows the traditions established fifty years ago, assuring the *Tzanhanim* a place at the forefront of any major operation. Given the small size of the country and its ongoing state of war, social attitudes regarding those who volunteer for such hazardous duty are always extremely positive, a fact that contributes to the paratroop recruit's morale and determination to succeed. Service in the *Tzanhanim*, which includes three compulsory years and an additional twenty-plus years of reserve duty, assures a man a unique place in Israeli society. Unlike most other countries, where special operations troops are regarded as somewhat "eccentric," in Israel the general staff is often composed of a majority of senior airborne officers.

IDF Pathfinders prepare to board a CH-53 chopper. (Samuel Katz)

IDF paratroopers hit a DZ as others are already moving out. (IDF)

The Tzanhanim and the IDF Armored Corps coordinate operations in Lebanon during strikes against Hizballah terrorists. (IDF)

Israeli paratroopers discussing the mission with tankers during operation in Lebanon. (IDF)

A paratrooper RTO and his C.O. wait for the next leg of a desert mission. (IDF)

Paratrooper training in Israel is a carefully-structured right of passage initially similar to that of any other modern army, then diverting to follow specific Israeli requirements. Volunteers must first pass a series of rigorous selection processes, including batteries of physical and psychological tests as well as personal interviews and careful security screenings. Upon selection to the brigade, the recruit enters a combined atmosphere of modern infantry training and airborne "tradition." First and foremost, he is hammered with the tenet, "Never leave a comrade in the field," which is branded on his psyche through long-range stretcher marches carrying "wounded" comrades. These grueling exercises begin with only a few kilometers, until eventually a training battalion will march over 90 kilometers in full combat gear to be awarded its red berets.

Considering that the IDF is regarded as a highly technological army, training facilities for the *Tzanhanim* are austere by any standard, and even the most permanent paratroop bases, such as the basic training facility, more resemble a Foreign Legion outpost than a western-style base such as Fort Bragg. Veteran paratroop commanders know that any wartime operations will be conducted without comfort facilities of any kind, and therefore keeping the paras accustomed to such conditions maintains their psychological "edge" should war break out. Throughout the greater part of the paratrooper's service, he can expect to live in a leaky tent, or in a sleeping bag under the desert stars.

Unlike in many western armies, the Israelis consider unit cohesiveness and camaraderie essential to successful operations. After twenty-five years of regular and reserve service, Israeli paras often muster out of the army along with many of the comrades they met as 18-year old volunteers. Upon completion of basic, an entire training battalion

During live-fire exercises in the desert, two members of a reconnaissance element negotiate an obstacle. (IDF)

During desert maneuvers in the Negev, a para M113 moves along a dirt road. (IDF)

will proceed to non-commissioned officers' school, from which exceptional candidates are selected for the six-month officers' training course. Simultaneously, "drill sergeants" are chosen to return to the basic training facility to shepherd green recruits. However, these NCOs, while highly skilled in small unit operations, have only scant abilities in parade ground formations and "spit and polish." Israeli troops as a whole are renown for their casual appearance. A salute is rarely seen outside of the basic training facility, and once paratroopers complete the "maslool," they will refer to their commanders, from sergeants to battalion leaders, by their first names. The IDF has always attracted a certain number of graduates of other European and American armies, and those foreign veterans are always shocked by the lack of surface discipline, while impressed by the level of combat discipline.

Reconnaissance paratroopers move through the snowy terrain of Mount Hermon, and then prepare a wounded comrade for evacuation.

Paras ready their chutes and gear for an early morning leap from a C-130. (IDF)

IDF paras care for a casualty in the snows of Mount Hermon. (IDF)

During a forty-kilometer trek across the desert, paratroopers show what they are made of as they negotiate the harsh Middle Eastern terrain. (IDF)

A para mortar man prepares to fire a 52mm round toward an enemy position. (IDF)

In southern Lebanon, two paratroopers stand on guard at a strategic tributary. (IDF)

The gentle fall to earth courtesy of a T-10. (IDF)

The true essence of wearing the red beret and silver jump wings—that moment at the door when the jump-master orders the stick out of the aircraft. (IDF)

Para pathfinders train in deploying from a CH-53 "Yasur" while under fire. (Samuel Katz)

Basic training includes the expected instruction in small arms usage, including the American M-16, Israeli Galil, Belgian MAG light machine-gun, Soviet-designed Rocket Propelled Grenade and a series of rifle and hand grenades. Small unit tactics are honed, certain squad members selected for APC driver training, while others are seconded to medic's courses to return later with their skills (Israeli medics are also fully armed combatants). Throughout this initial training period, the paratroopers also receive historical lectures on the Airborne Corps' past operations, both successes and failures. Quite interestingly, officers from the IDF Education Corps also instruct the recruits in modern state history as well as biblical history, with a view toward solidifying the paratrooper's link to his country. It is not unusual for an airborne unit to be halted in the middle of a long range forced march, so that an education officer (often a comely female lieutenant) can recall a biblical battle on the very spot where the recruits are standing.

Constant training is the essence of success for the Israeli paratroopers. (Samuel Katz)

Paratroopers deploy with tanks clearing a mine-field during training in the Negev Desert. (IDF)

Para recon troopers race to an awaiting chopper following operations in southern Lebanon. (IDF)

After a successful counter-terrorist strike against Hizbollah gunmen in Lebanon, paratroopers head for their transportation for a safe trip home.

Two female paratroopers prepare to lay a wreath at the IDF Paratrooper Memorial. (Samuel Katz)

Parachute training, though essential to the *Tzanhan*'s skill resume, is actually considered a short respite in the basic training schedule. The airborne training school at Tel Nof is a much smaller model of America's Fort Benning, but the rigorous instruction and equipment is much the same, with the Israelis utilizing a modified T-10 parachute called "The Sabra," as well as the steerable MC1-1B. Although the American C-130 Hercules has become the standard drop aircraft, the Israel Air Force still maintains a large fleet of C-47s, and paratroopers often find themselves jumping from these ghosts of airborne history as they complete their first five drops and earn their silver wings in a solemn parade ceremony before the Paratrooper's Memorial.

Women also play a crucial role in the IDF Airborne Corps. Although the Israelis have not yet been persuaded that women should serve as front line combatants in any unit, company "clerks" in the *Tzanhanim* are always young female volunteers, sharing the adverse conditions of basic training and field bivouacs. These young women provide a certain "den mother" aspect in their concern for the psychological and social welfare of the recruits, while also participating in grueling forced marches, which adds a certain, "If she can do it, I can," impetus for the exhausted troops. In addition, all parachute riggers at the Airborne school are females, a tradition established long ago when IDF psychologists determined that their level of maturity and sense of responsibility toward "the boys" would insure attention to technical detail. Female riggers must themselves be parachute-qualified, and quality control is assured as they are randomly selected to jump with a parachute they have just packed.

The IDF has never had the luxury of being a peacetime army, and volunteers for special operations units such as the *Tzanhanim* know that "their time will come." Unlike most western nations, where a paratrooper accepts the fact that he will most likely never fire a shot in anger, an Israeli para volunteers with the knowledge that sooner or later he will be in action. Training and field operations continue unabated throughout reserve duty (often as much as 45 days per year), and it is not unusual for a gnarled "old" para of forty to find himself lying in ambush facing the Hezbollah in southern Lebanon.

When a young Israeli chooses silver wings and red beret, he also chooses a life replete with hardship, danger and the certain reward of knowing that he is one of the special operations elite.

Steven Hartov served in the IDF Airborne Corps and Military Intelligence. He is the author of the novels, The Heat Of Ramadan and The Nylon Hand Of God, as well as numerous non-fiction articles on military subjects. He is the director of the Airborne Operations Group, an organization of military parachutists.

The author (left) and IDF Lieutenant-Colonel (Res.) Shaul Dori lay a wreath at the Israeli Memorial to fallen Paratroopers (note the KIAs etched in bronze plates).

Israel Defense Forces Special Operations And Counter-Terrorist Units

FLOTILLA 13: The IDF/Navy's naval commando element was created in 1948, and has participated in hundreds of naval special warfare and counter-terrorist operations, including the sinking of the Egyptian Navy flagship, the *R.E.N.S. Emir Farouk* on October 21, 1948; the assault on Green Island in July 1969; the February 21, 1973 raid against PFLP bases in Tripoli, Lebanon; the April 9, 1973 "Operation Spring of Youth" raid against Black September and *el-Fatah* targets in the heart of Beirut. According to foreign reports, naval commando forces secured a beachhead for a force of *Mossad* agents and *Sayeret Mat'kal* commandos on April 16, 1988, on the shores of Tunis, prior to the assassination of PLO deputy commander Abu Jihad. According to reports, naval commandos secured the beachhead for the *Sayeret Golani* force tasked with attacking Jibril's lair at al-Na'ameh on December 9, 1988. The unit's last operation, a raid against Hizballah units in southern Lebanon on the night of September 4-5, 1997, ended disastrously when twelve Flotilla 13 operators were killed in a well-planned ambush.

MISTA'ARAVIM: Figuratively "The Arabists," this unit, formed during the Palestinian *Intifadah*, was tasked with apprehending and neutralizing key—and heavily armed!—elements of the Palestinian uprising; later the unit was an instrumental weapon in the war against Hamas and its key operatives. One unit, known as *Duvdevan* (or "Cherry") operated in the West Bank and is still operational in the villages and towns not turned over to the Palestinian Authority (PA). *Shimshon* (or "Samson") operated in the Gaza Strip until it was handed over the Yasir Arafat's PA. The men of this unit all masquerade as local Arabs, and produce weapons from their indigenous clothing before striking out at their targets. The Israeli National Police Border Guard also maintains an undercover unit, and it is known by its acronym of *Ya'mas.*

SAYERET GOLANI: Known by their affectionate military nickname of *Ha'Namer Ha'Me'ufaf,* or "Flying Tigers," the reconnaissance force from the 1st Golani Infantry Brigade is one of the more effective conventional commando forces in the IDF's order of battle. Excellent shock troops in battle against Syrian commandos on top of the Golan Heights in 1967 and 1973, and against Palestinian guerrillas in Lebanon in 1982, they are also a unit with a rich counter-terrorist heritage. During the dark days of the 1967-70 War of Attrition, the "Flying Tigers" fought a bitter counter-insurgency campaign against Palestinian guerrillas in the notorious *Fatahland* region between the Lebanese, Syrian and Israeli frontiers. In 1974, *Sayeret Golani* commandos fought back Jibril's suicide commandos in Kiryat Shmoneh, and along the beaches of

Nahariya; the unit also played a significant role during the IDF's spectacular "Operation Yonatan" rescue of 103 hostages from Entebbe, on July 4, 1976. One of *Sayeret Golani's* most infamous operations was the December 9, 1988, raid on Ahmed Jibril's lair at al-Na'amah.

SAYERET MAT'KAL: The highly classified, ultra-top-secret, General Staff Reconnaissance Unit was formed in 1957 as a super elite reconnaissance force to be despatched deep behind enemy lines to conduct intelligence-gathering operations; they were to be a mission impossible type force known to only a select few in the IDF General Staff. Their special talents, however, also landed them a unique role as counter-terrorists. In 1968, a *Sayeret Mat'kal* force launched a retaliatory raid against Beirut International Airport, in which thirteen Middle East Airlines aircraft were destroyed. *Sayeret Mat'kal* also participated in the May 1972 rescue of a hijacked Sabena airliner to Lod (in which the commandos dressed up as mechanics in white coveralls); the assassination of three of Black September's top commanders in "Operation Spring of Youth;" the rescue bids at Ma'alot and at the Savoy Hotel in Tel Aviv; and, of course, spearheading the rescue operation at Entebbe under the command of Lieutenant-Colonel Yonatan "Yoni" Netanyahu. According to foreign reports, the unit was responsible for the April 1988 assassination of PLO deputy commander Abu Jihad, and the July 1989 abduction of *Hizbollah* commander Sheikh Abdel Karim Obeid. Interestingly enough, both the Prime Minister of Israel, Benjamin Netanyahu, and the leader of the opposition labor party, Ehud Barak, are both *Sayeret Mat'kal* veterans, though Barak was both unit commander and eventual IDF Chief of Staff.

SAYERET TZANHANIM: The reconnaissance force of the IDF's conscript paratroop brigade, *Sayeret Tzanhanim* has participated in some of the most bitterly fought battles in Israeli history—from the Golan Heights to the urban squalor of Suez City and Beirut. They have participated in their share of spectacular counter-terrorist operations, including the 1968 raid on Beirut International Airport, "Spring of Youth," "Entebbe," and other operations that are still classified to this day.

UNIT 669: The IAF's elite aeromedical evacuation unit, Unit 669 is tasked with rescuing downed pilots stranded deep behind enemy lines, as well as additional heliborne special operations involving medical evacuations.

YA'MA'M: Acronym for Special Police Unit, the *Ya'ma'm* is the National Police Border Guard's specialized hostage-rescue unit, built much like Germany's infamous GSG-9.

11th NL Airmobile Brigade

Walter Böhm

A Company of the 13th Airmobile Infantry Battalion "Shock Troops Regiment" is waiting in a small forest in Drawsko-Pommerski, Poland, for the arrival of the transport helicopter that would take them to the operation zone. The 11th NL Airmobile Brigade has three infantry battalions, one battalion consisting of 500 soldiers.

The proven 7.62mm MAG is the principal weapon of the Dutch infantry, the weapon is also used by the US Marine Corps and other NATO nations.

Twilight descends over the forests of Pommern, in Poland, as an icy wind blows in the faces of the soldiers of the 13th NL Airmobile Infantry Battalion "Shock Troops Regiment," who are lying in position on the edge of the forest on an evening. A monotonous throbbing can be heard from afar, that becomes quickly louder. Two Dutch CH-47D Chinook transport helicopters float into the clearing in the forest at tree-top height. The icy wind is increased by the rotor blades of the helicopters. While one Chinook hovers above the forest setting, the second lands in a clearing. Two vehicles detach themselves from the edge of the forest and drive to the middle of the forest clearing below the helicopter hovering in the air. The soldiers fix the Mercedes-Benz all-terrain vehicle to the external hooks of the transport helicopter with belts. After the loading hatch of the second Chinook is opened, and acting on a visual signal, the soldiers of the 13th Airmobile Infantry Battalion hasten to the helicopter with Zodiac rubber dinghies, in which they have packed small-arms, anti-tank weapons and back-packs, and then quickly disappear inside. When the loading hatch is closed the helicopter immediately lifts off and flies away at tree-top height, shortly after this further Chinooks fly in and take off the all-terrain vehicles and the rest of the Battalion.

This airborne operation by parts of the 11th NL Airmobile Brigade was one of the highlights of the "Rhino Drawsko 97" maneuvers in April 1997, on the Polish Army Training Ground at Drawsko Pommerskie near Stettin. In this maneuver the Dutch Army, together with units of the 13th NL Mechanized Brigade, tested the advantages and strengths of an airmobile troop that stress speed, distance and mobility.

The three infantry battalions of the 11th NL Airmobile Brigade have the latest equipment of the Dutch Army, such as Gortex DPM-pattern jackets in British camouflage style as well as the Canadian C 7 Diemaco automatic rifle.

Most members of the 11th NL Airmobile Brigade are up to twenty-six years old and are regular soldiers with terms of up to thirty months. From the start of training every airmobile soldier works together with a "Buddy," this "two-man team" has proved to be a reliable system for the special operations assignments often assigned to the Brigade.

FLEXIBILITY AND MOBILITY

The Airmobile Brigade consists of highly-trained and dedicated soldiers selected from the very best of the Dutch armed forces. Helicopters ensure the rapid deployment of Airmobile Brigade troops and provide transport of weapons, equipment, food and other supplies. In addition and if required, the brigade may deploy attack helicopters to protect and provide fire support to ground troops. Light all-terrain vehicles (Mercedes-Benz), portable anti-tank weapons and state-of-the-art communications equipment make up the combat power of the brigade.

BACKGROUND

The international security situation has undergone dramatic changes over the past few years. After the dissolution of the Iron Curtain, world peace appeared to be at hand. Unfortunately, this expectation was not

The red beret is the headgear of the Dutch airmobile soldiers. The falcon on the uniform of the soldiers of the 11th NL Airmobile Brigade was chosen as the symbol for the airmobile brigade because this bird can be found all over the world, has keen eyes, and is a flying predator.

fulfilled. Numerous regional conflicts and crisis emerged. The Gulf War, political tension in the republics of the former Soviet Union, civil wars in African countries and, of course, the crisis in the former Yugoslavia are the most well-known examples. Participation in peace operations requires a rapidly deployable armed force with a high level of mobility that can moreover be deployed all over the world, even in barely accessible terrain. In short, units capable of providing an optimal contribution to crisis management tasks. The Royal Netherlands Army's Airmobile Brigade was set up to this end in 1993.

HISTORY

11th Brigade was formed on 14th November 1960. Initially named "11th Infantry Brigade," five years later it became the "11th Mechanized Infantry Brigade," which remained unchanged in name and mission until

Every company of the airmobile infantry battalions has an FN 7.62mm sniper gun as well as a number of anti-tank weapon systems such as the AT-4, that can also be used successfully against bunker targets.

In order to be able to operate independent of ground hinderances such as water-courses, this company of the 13th Airmobile Infantry Battalion carries Zodiac boats with it during the "Rhino Drawsko 97" maneuver in Poland, that were also used to transport weapons.

The NATO MND plans that, with the national transport helicopter, every brigade of the MND Central can move a fighting battalion at one time. The 11th NL Airborne Brigade is a part of the MND Central. Apart from the Cougar transport helicopter, the Boeing CH-47D Chinook transport helicopter is also used for moving troops. The CH-47D Chinooks belong to 298 Squadron Tactical Helicopter Group and are stationed at Soestberg Air Base (NL).

The transport helicopters are a decisive force in operations. For moving troops the THG (Tactical Helicopter Group) supports the 11th NL Airmobile Brigade with thirteen CH-47D Chinooks and seven Cougar transport helicopters.

The airborne mobility gives the 11th NL Airmobile Brigade the possibility of moving their fighting battalions to the right point at the decisive moment, as here in an operation during the "Rhino Drawsko 97" exercise in Poland.

ORGANIZATION

The 11th NL Airmobile Brigade is made up to three infantry battalions, the 11th Airmobile Infantry Battalion (Grenadiers and Rifle Guards Regiment), the 12th Airmobile Infantry Battalion (Van Heutz Regiment) and the 13th Airmobile Infantry Battalion (Shock Troops Regiment), with various support troops, some 2,700 personnel in all. The three battalions consist of three infantry companies and one headquarters and combat service support company. Each company comprises four platoons. The helicopters used by the brigade belong to the Royal Netherlands Air Force Tactical Helicopter Group (RNAF/THG). They are

1992, when the airmobile role was adopted in the light of changing international, especially European, security environment. 11th NL Airmobile Brigade operates primarily as a part of the NATO's MND Central (Multinational Division Central), but it can also contribute to the Main Defence Forces in Central Europe. A third mission is to participate in peace-keeping missions under the flag of the United Nations or other international organizations. A battalion-size unit can be deployed at any one time at short notice. During the period January 1994 until July 1995, the three battalions of the Brigade have been committed as a part of the UN Protection Force (UNPROFOR) in Bosnia.

Airborne loading operation of soldiers of the 13th Airmobile Infantry Battalion during the "Rhino Drawsko 97" maneuver in Poland. The battle proven Boeing CH-47D transport helicopter is powered by two turbo-shaft Allied Signal 55-L-714A turbines and can take thirty-one fully-equipped infantrymen.

The transport helicopters are the "wings" of the 11th NL Airmobile Brigade. The Boeing CH-47D Chinook is equipped with three hooks for carrying underslung loads. The fore and aft hooks are each capable of carrying 9,072 kilograms and the center hook 12,700 kilograms. This CH-47D Chinook intends to take two all-terrain vehicles of the anti-tank platoon of the 13th Airmobile Infantry Battalion into the operation zone.

The 11th NL Airmobile Brigade is subordinate to the NATO MND Central (Multinational Division Central). During the first field training exercise, "Cold Grouse 95" in Denmark, the 11th NL Airmobile Brigade had no transport helicopters of their own and relied on the air transport capacity of other NATO members. This photograph features a German CH-53G transport helicopter loading a Landrover of the 12th NL Infantry Battalion (Van Heutsz Regiment).

flown by air force crews. The Air Force and the Airmobile Brigade naturally work in close cooperation. The three infantry battalions constitute the brigade's combat units consisting of some five hundred servicemen. In addition to these combat units, the brigade has support units facilitating the deployment of the airmobile infantry personnel. The support units are independent companies ranging in strength from 100 to 250 personnel. They are responsible for supplies and equipment and are assigned to a mortar, supply, maintenance, engineer and medical company, and headquarters and headquarters company respectively.

- 11th Mortar Company (Airmobile) provides the brigade with fire support by means of twelve 120mm mortars. The maximum range of these heavy weapons is 8,100 meters. Intense fire can be delivered within four minutes of weaponry and personnel landing at a forward LZ by helicopter.
- Engineer Company (Airmobile) has the personnel and equipment for putting up or removing obstacles, or moving soil for protected positions. Its personnel also function as plumbers, carpenters and electricians for the brigade units. To this end, the company is equipped with small construction machines, inflatable reconnaissance vessels, motorized chain saws, mine detectors, bow drills and various hand tools, making the force completely self-reliant for most of it needs.
- 11th Maintenance Company (Airmobile) repairs the brigade's motorcycles, all-terrain vehicles, trucks, weaponry, instruments and electronic equipment. The company has its own repair facilities, for which it supplies the parts itself. Recovering or storing broken-down equipment, both on the premises of the barracks, in the field and during action constitutes one of the tasks of the maintenance company.
- 11th Supply Company (Airmobile) provides the 2,700 troops of the brigade with ammunition, food, fuel, spare parts and equipment. For

The Bölkow 105CB light helicopter of THG is used for reconnaissance and evacuation of wounded personnel.

this purpose the Supply Company has at its disposal nine tank trucks, with 7,000 liter capacity each and over seventy trucks, some of which are equipped with loading cranes. The company has twelve mobile field kitchens at its disposal for food preparations.
- 11th Medical Company (Airmobile) can set up two field dressing stations for the treatment of the wounded and sick. Life-saving surgery can be performed in the field dressing stations, which are also equipped for dental and psychiatric care. Fore more complicated surgery or more extensive medical treatment, patients are transported elsewhere by ambulance or helicopter.
- Headquarters and Headquarters Company comprises the Brigade staff. This company sets up the Brigade Command Post and takes care of its security. In addition, the Brigade signal platoon provides the required wire and radio communications between the brigade units and the command post.

301 Squadron Tactical Helicopter Group (THG) has twelve AH-64 Apache combat helicopters leased from the US Army. It is planned to buy nine NAH-64D "Longbow" Apache helicopters, refitted for combat, in the future.

FIRE POWER

The characteristic feature of the Airmobile Brigade is the speed with which it can move its arms which have considerable fire power. Apart from small arms, the brigade has heavy 120mm mortars, light 81mm mortars, Stinger anti-aircraft missiles and AT-4, TOW and Dragon anti-tank systems. For delivering mortar fire the brigade uses sophisticated laser equipment with which enemy targets can be illuminated and the distance to targets measured. Weapons are not only airmobile, but fitted in such a way that they are man portable with exception of the 120mm mortars.

COMMUNICATIONS

Using satellite stations, the Global Positioning System (GPS) enables military personnel to determine their position with great accuracy. For the communications with headquarters and between platoons and companies, the brigade has sophisticated portable communications equipment at its disposal.

VEHICLES

Soon it is hoped, the Airmobile Brigade will have special light all-terrain vehicles, the so-called Airmobile Special Vehicles, which can be transported by air. Combat readiness is more important feature for these vehicles than comfort. Among other things they may be used to evacuate the wounded, carry out reconnaissance duties, transport radio equipment or weapon systems and supply food and ammunition. Until such time as these vehicles become available, the Brigade uses soft-top terrain vehicles.

HELICOPTERS

The Helicopters of the Tactical Helicopter Groups Royal Netherlands Air Force (THG/RNLAF) are the workhorse of the 11th NL Airmobile Brigade. The Bölkow 105 CB, a so-called "light utility helicopter," twenty-eight of which are presently operational, is used for reconnaissance, command and control purposes and for medical transport. Troop transport and transport of equipment is carried out by

Because of its weaponry, with Hellfire anti-tank rockets (up to sixteen), Stinger air-to-air missiles (up to four), 2.75 inch purpose submunitions, 30mm cannon, the AH-64A Apache is an attack helicopter. The principal task of the Apache with the 11th NL Airmobile Brigade is to ensure combat support for the transport helicopters into the operation zone, and to provide fire protection for the landed ground troops.

The "Rhino Drawsko 97" maneuvers was the first battle maneuver of Dutch troops in Poland, on the troops exercise ground at Drawsko Pommerski in April 1997. Soldiers of the 13th Airmobile Infantry Battalion were used, as well as parts of the THG, in order to test the capability of the new equipment of the 11th NL Airmobile Brigade in use against a mechanically strong enemy equipped with tanks. The photographs show soldiers of the 13th Airmobile Infantry Battalion "Shock Troops" during the "Rhino Drawsko 97" maneuvers.

seventeen Cougar and thirteen Chinook transport helicopters. The Cougar, with a payload of 10,000 kilograms, is also used for resupply and medical transport. The Chinook has a payload and sling load of 10,000 kilograms which makes it highly suitable for carrying out humanitarian aid tasks. The thirty Apache armed helicopters cover transports on enemy territory, perform reconnaissance tasks and give fire support to ground combat units when necessary. The transport and armed helicopters have been procured specially for the Airmobile Brigade. As from the beginning of 1996, the first seven modernized CH-47D Chinooks purchased from Canada will be taken into use gradually. The introduction of six new Chinooks follows as from 1998.

The AS-532 U2 Cougar Mk II is expected in 1996 and 1997. The first delivery of the NAH-64D Longbow Apache is scheduled for the autumn of 1998. As of 1996, however twelve machines will be leased. With each new Apache entering service, one leased machine will be returned. All helicopters are expected to be operational by the year 2002.

TACTICS AND "AIRMOBILE MECHANIZATION"

The great strength of the 11th NL Airmobile Brigade is the combination of light infantry and airborne mobility through the use of transport helicopters that, according to the type of deployment required, can act fast and flexibly. Through the transport helicopters the Brigade can appear with surprise and concentration from any direction and free their own threatened troops from dangerous situations. Other tasks of the armed helicopters are reconnaissance, fire control of nearby air support or indirect fire and escorting of transport helicopters.

The FN FAL 7.62mm rifle was used by elements of the unit until the introduction of the C 7 Diemaco automatic rifle.

Every one of the three infantry battalions has the Stinger air defense system against the threat from the air.

The 11th NL Airmobile Brigade can carry out airborne operations directly from the "staging area" into the operation zone as well as through "Forward Operating Bases" (FOB). The average range of the helicopters at present however is only about 120 kilometers, so that operational distance is limited. For the future they are trying to bridge over airborne distances of up 300 kilometers because, from a tactical operational point of view, only this distance will bring real advantages with regard to the reaction ability. This distance could be especially important for the new strategy of overcoming crises, or for destroyed infrastructure airborne mobility is also necessary for shorter distances. Speed can be used to the optimum through the operative and tactical mobility of helicopter use, the troops can be taken quickly and in large numbers to operation zones. The 11th NL Airmobile Brigade has defense capability and, with the AH-64 Apache combat helicopters, attack capability, as well. The Apache combat helicopters are the brigade's ultimate resource for directed firepower, and can be used both against ground targets as well as air-to-air targets, day and night under all weather conditions. The Apache combat helicopter is an attack helicopter that has a long range and aircraft cannons and rocket systems with modern fire control techniques. This helicopter enables ground troops to gain ground and support advances. With the AH-64 Apache combat helicopters the 11th NL Airmobile Brigade is in the position of carrying out airborne mechanized operations—they have the ability to maneuver in the air and to fight ground troops and helicopters of the opponent mainly from the air. Because of its ability to combine transport, combat and reconnaissance missions into such a neat cohesive package, 11th NL Airmobile Brigade is truly one of the most capable fighting formations today.

Contact with the helicopters of the THG (Tactical Helicopter Group) is maintained by the ground troops through wireless communications. Teams (Air Control Party) of the THG are subordinated to the combat troops in order to ensure air support by AH-64 Apache attack helicopters if necessary, or to accompany the transport helicopters to the rendezvous point.

Because of the lack of armor protection the 11th NL Airmobile Brigade has considerable anti-tank ability, such as the TOW anti-tank system mounted on the MBAT (Mercedes-Benz anti-tank) all-terrain vehicle. The MB (Mercedes-Benz) has complete airborne ability and is transported by the transport helicopters as an external load into the operation zone. Apart from being a weapons carrier the vehicle also serves the combat battalions for transporting wireless appliances, ammunitions, material and food, as well as for carrying away the wounded.

A Landrover of the 12th Airmobile Infantry Battalion equipped with a MAG 7.62mm machine gun, during the "Cold Grouse 95" maneuvers in Denmark. The Landrover was replaced with the new Mercedes-Benz all-terrain vehicle.

The light, mobile infantry battalions of the 11th NL Airmobile Brigade are especially suitable for the new strategy of overcoming crisis for the UNO, NATO or WEU, because the highly mobile infantry units can also be used in areas with destroyed infrastructure.

"Desert Commandos/Desert Aviators"
Jordanian Special Operations Capabilities Today

Samuel M. Katz

Flying over a fertile area near the northern frontier with Israel and Jordan, a flight of four Special Operations Squadron UH-1s use a desert roadway as a guide toward their target.

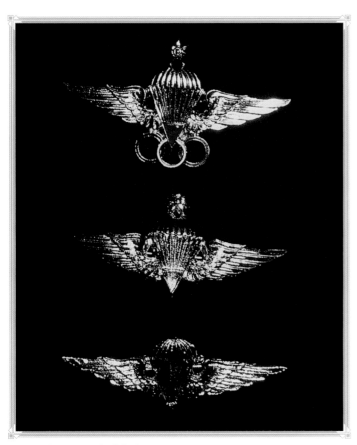

Jordanian parachutist wings

Just before dawn, on an already sizzling valley in the desert near Amman, the hazy skies to the west reveal an ominous approach. Although far from being visible, the pounding of the rotor-blade cadence of the choppers is unmistakable. The noise reverberates through the valley and through anyone in the desert. As the pounding crisp thuds of the approaching helicopters grows louder and more threatening, six visible olive drab dots appear over the horizon. They are flying fast and flying low and they are grouped in a tight, almost shoulder-to-shoulder formation. As the choppers come in close, another chopper shoots in from the left in a ground-hugging swoop of daredevil flying. The UH-1 is only on the ground a split-second, but that is more than enough time for a force of heavily camouflaged rangers to jump off and assume firing positions. With red smoke grenades indicating the LZ as "hot," the rest of the formation comes in for a landing wary of being caught in the middle of a cross-fire. The soldiers on the ground are firing their M-16 assault rifles and M-60 light machine guns in fusillades of well-placed firepower provide maximum cover to the incoming birds. Door-gunners hanging out of the incoming choppers, too, unleash barrages of 7.62mm ordnance that turns sections of the desert into a churned up cloud of dust and debris.

For fifty years, the Jordanian military has possessed the reputation as being the most professional in the Middle East. British-trained, American-supplied and deep in tradition and skill, the Jordanian military traces its origin to the Great Arab Revolt of 1916 under the command of Sharif Hussein Ibn Ali; the nucleus of the legendary Arab Legion was a dedicated force of irregular desert warriors who accompanied Amir Abdullah when he arrived in Jordan in 1920. Today, equipped with everything from Khaled main battle tanks to F-16 fighter bombers, that reputation continues, but the modern Jordanian military possesses a trump card in its national defense equation—the Royal Jordanian Special Forces.

Brigadier-General Majid Megableh, commander of the SF School, looks on as Special Forces free-fallers board an RJAF Special Operations Squadron UH-1.

High above the agricultural hub of northwestern Jordan, a flight of UH-1s heads north toward the Syrian frontier.

Like most Arab militaries following the 1948 war with Israel, the Jordanian Army did not invest heavily in special operations units during its formative years of development; commando units, after all, were a luxury when faced with the daunting challenge of fielding a well-equipped and highly-trained conventional army and air force. By the early 1960s, however, the term "special forces" had entered the international military vernacular and the Jordan Arab Army was determined to maintain an elite entity of its own. The first jump-qualified paratroopers received their wings in April 1963, forming the cornerstone of a company-size airborne element, and in 1969 the first Special Forces Battalion was created. British-trained, the hand-picked commandos in the battalion saw extensive fighting against Palestinian guerrilla forces in the Black September civil war of 1970; few Palestinian guerrillas who fought against the battalion in the camps inside Amman, as well as in the notorious Wachdat area, will ever forget their tenacious firepower and close-quarter zeal. In 1971 the Special Forces became a brigade and was tasked with maintaining a "conventionally unconventional" strategic edge with the elongated frontier with Israel (as well as the borders with Syria and Iraq). In 1976, following a failed attempt by PFLP terrorists to seize the Intercontinental Hotel in Amman and an uncoordinated counter-assault by Jordanian security forces, counter-terrorism also become the domain of the special forces.

The Middle East is a very different place than it was at the time of the Intercontinental Hotel attack, however, and the Royal Jordanian Special Forces today is a very different unit than it was twenty-one years ago. Commanded by His Royal Highness Brigadier Abdullah Bin al-Hussein, a Sandhurst graduate and an energetic officer of boundless energy and vision, the Royal Jordanian Special Forces have grown in their abilities and mandate. Over the course of his command of the unit,

On the flight deck, a mini-armada of Royal Jordanian Air Force Special Operations Squadrons UH-1s line up for take-off.

His Royal Highness Brigadier Abdullah Bin al-Hussein has seen to it that the special forces are a breeding ground of innovative military thought; he has instilled in its ranks an operational doctrine of absolute professionalism. In fact, in late 1996, the importance of the special forces to overall national security of the country was reinforced with the creation of the Royal Jordanian Special Operations Command (RJSOC)—combining the Special Forces and Royal Guard under one-joint command umbrella.

The Royal Jordanian Special Forces' multi-task mission mandate consists of: acting as the armed forces strategic reserve during full-scale military deployments; executing unconventional warfare missions and counter-insurgency operations; executing internal security assignments and counter-terrorism missions; counter-sabotage assignments both inside Jordan, as well as in the defense of Jordanian installations throughout the world; riot-control; "conventional" and "unconventional"

Although a relic in some armies, the UH-1 is considered a natural for the hard flying of the desert—it is durable, fast, powerful and, perhaps most importantly, reliable.

A RJAF Special Operations Squadron UH-1 lands on the desert near Zarqa.

A force of Royal Jordanian Special Forces operators deploy in the desert from a Special Operations Squadron UH-1.

A UH-1 prepares to take-off in the desert, loaded with its compliment of Jordanian special forces personnel.

military operations beyond the scope and abilities of the "conventional" Royal Jordanian military; to train other units of the armed forces in the art of special operations warfare, such as ranger and air-mobile operations, airborne operations, as well as other facets of the special forces regimen; and, most importantly, counter-terrorism and hostage-rescue assignments inside Jordan, as well as around the region, and around the world (skymarshals securing Royal Jordanian flights are taken from the ranks of the Special Forces).

The very heart of the RJSOC is the Special Forces Brigade which is divided into a Special Forces Group, an Airborne Battalion, a Ranger Battalion, Airborne Artillery Battalion, and the Special Forces School; supporting these battalion-size units are an anti-aircraft company (armed primarily with hand-launched weapons such as the Stinger surface-to-air missile); an air operations company; and, an anti-tank company, armed primarily with high-speed Land Rovers, ideal vehicles for the desert, armed with TOW missiles and heavy machine guns.

It takes a special type of soldier to not only endure and master the elements of the desert, but to race across a clearing wearing a backpack laden down with forty-kilograms of equipment, and fire his weapon as a commando is trained to do. Soldiers wishing to one day wear the gold jump wings on their chest and sport the maroon beret must pass a grueling series of physical and psychological examinations before even being allowed to formally volunteer. The objective of this often back-breaking selection process is to ensure that when a class of future operators commences, that only those with the stamina, spirit and psychological capacities will engage in the many months of special forces instruction. Initially, special forces instructors hope to build a "commando" mind-set into the recruit, before the technical aspects of special warfare can be taught and skills honed and perfected. The physical training a volunteer endures is meant to increase his aggressiveness, as well as build his self-confidence and the trust and compatibility of his fellow recruits. The first phase of commando training includes: (1) basic military drill; (2) physical training and forced

The Royal Jordanian Air Force's primary gunship—the AH-1 Cobra.

The AH-1 Cobras of the Royal Jordanian Air Force are often called upon to support Special Forces deployments.

With its door-mounted M-60 light machine guns at a ready, a Royal Jordanian Air Force Special Operations Squadron UH-1 chopper awaits a mission.

marches; (3) navigation, topography, and map-reading; (4) first-aid and emergency medical care; (5) basic signals and communications; (6) basic weapons training; (7) anti-tank weapons; (8) mountain warfare training; (9) amphibious operations; (10) extensive martial arts, hand-to-hand fighting, bayonet and Kukri training; (11) calling in air and artillery strikes; (12) anti-aircraft training (heavy machine guns and shoulder-fired surface-to-air missiles); (13) NBC training; (14) parachute training, including day and night jumps; (15) anti-riot training; (16) squad leadership skills; and, (17) specialized support training for combined arms operations.

Upon graduation from the Special Forces School, the commando enters a new and equally as lengthy phase of instruction where his individual and newly mastered skills are translated into squad, platoon and company level exercises. During this phase of the operator's instruction, he is taught the A-to-Zs of squad and platoon level tactics; tactical deployments in diverse terrain; combined arms training with different units and support services; tactical parachutist training; urban warfare skills; airborne operations deploying from both fixed wing and rotary aircraft; patrolling, ambush and infiltration techniques; deception operations; advanced NBC instruction; anti-airborne operations; and, field support operations. Graduates of the "basic" commando course, operators who have mastered over a year's worth of special forces curriculum, are full-fledged members of the airborne battalion. The best soldiers within the battalion are, following several years of service with an exemplary record, afforded the opportunity to volunteer into the Special Forces Battalion.

A basic catchword around the special forces is "challenge"—the challenge to excel on the training ground, the challenge to excel in battle, and the challenge to remain the nation's cutting-edge military force. In fact, a Jordanian-brand of martial arts, an offensive means of cold-killing and sentry-removal, is called "Sijal"—the Arabic-word for challenge. On a parade ground in Zarqa, Brigadier-General Majid, the jovial commander of the Special Forces School who speaks both Hebrew and Serbo-Croation, stands by a reviewing stand as a small squad of troopers

armed with razor sharp Kukris and bone-breaking sticks of bamboo go through the motions of a Sijal demonstrations. The crushing blows and wind-snapping swings are very real, as are the bruises and gashes on the bodies of many of the operators. During one demonstration, in which a sergeant with a barrel for a chest and tree-trunks for arms literally removes five "sentries" single-handedly, Brigadier-General Majid comments that one of his men might be hurt. The soldier, hit across the arms with a bamboo pole, is bleeding heavily and his left hand is mangled. "It is nothing but a scratch," the brigadier comments, as an endearing smile is produced at the corner of his mouth. "Sijal challenges the soldiers not to be scared and not to be daunted or slowed down by being unarmed. It is something that we instill into each of our soldiers."

The concept of the commandos always being pushed, and pushing themselves, toward excellence, is one of the most important aspects of Prince Abdullah's command of the special forces. He has seen to it that great resources are invested into the special forces, and those investments have reaped untold dividends. Jordanian Special Forces operators shoot more, train harder and parachute more than perhaps any other special operations force in the region; there is a powerful wind-tunnel simulator helps endear HALO paratroopers to the gravity-tug of free fall parachuting, and paratroopers will have often jumped from either a transport plane or chopper before the morning's sun has risen. Parachuting, in fact, is a passion of the special forces and of Prince Abdullah.

The Royal Jordanian Special Forces routinely train with the Green Berets of U.S. Special Forces, U.S. Marines (such as the recent "Operation Early Victory 97" exercises), British special operations forces, and commando forces from the friendly Arab nations in the regions. The international contacts are important. Special forces officers and NCOs alike are encouraged to study the tactics, equipment and deployment of other similar units around the world and, where applicable, to adopt them to the unit's tasks and assignments. The Royal Jordanian Special Forces have also been deployed overseas, in international peace-keeping missions. Their largest deployment was as part of UNPROFOR in Bosnia. Over 3,000 Jordanian soldiers were sent to the former Yugoslavia, many of them coming from the Special Forces Brigade, and many of them found themselves in the middle of no-man's land, between Serb and Croat lines, and often in the center of a murderous cross-fire. Several special forces operators were seriously hurt in the United Nations effort. They were applauded for their heroism, tenacity and courage under fire.

One of the RJSOC's most important duties is counter-terrorism and hostage-rescue and the special forces element tasked with this mission, "Special Operations Unit 71," is among the world's finest. Formed in the aftermath of "Skyjack Sunday" and the brutal-fighting of the fighting of *Ailul al-Aswad,* the brutal fighting of "Black September 1970" and subsequently in 1971, SOU 71 small, though highly cohesive force of operators who would train specifically for the fight against terrorism and hostage-rescue. These were the best fighters in the special forces — the smartest and toughest soldiers, those with the strongest elements of command and those with the natural skills of innovation and improvisation that are a must in the world of a special forces operators. When the PFLP took over the Intercontinental Hotel in Amman in 1978, it was the special forces' counter-terrorist operators that went into action. The battle for the Intercontinental was fierce and close-quarter. Two special forces operators and seven civilians were killed; three terrorists were also killed.

SOU 71 is believed to consist of between 100-200 operators and made up solely of volunteers. Before a commando can volunteer into the unit, he is of course special forces qualified having undergone basic training and more likely than not training at the hands of U.S. Special Forces or British Special Air Service instructors. The volunteer must also first pass a special unit medical examination, IQ test, Physical Training test, Endurance Test, and Psychological Test. The actual training regimen for SOU 71 consists of (1) physical fitness training; (2) sharp-shooting skills; (3) explosives and EOD instruction; (4) first aid and emergency medical technician training; (5) climbing, and rappelling; (6) heliborne insertion and extraction; (7) assault training—performing rescues against targets like aircraft, buildings, vehicles and ships; (8) special night assault training; and, (9) sniper training. Renown for their dark blue fatigues and British DPM pattern bullet-proof vests, the unit's equipment consists of the ubiquitous German-made Heckler and Koch MP5 family of 9mm submachine guns, Steyr special police sniper rifles, 12-gauge shotguns, and Browning Hi-Power automatics. There isn't a specialized task in Jordan, or the region, that the Royal Jordanian Special Forces, with SOU 71 in the vanguard, cannot handle.

Another special operations workhorse of the Royal Jordanian Special Operations Squadron—the Aérospatiale AS.332M Super Puma. Seen here, the Super Puma awaits a mission on the ground at Al-Jafr.

A busy day on the tarmac at King Abdullah Air Force base at Marka—C-130s are readied for flight while UH-1s are secured for take-off.

In the air, too, the Royal Jordanian Special Operations Command is prepared to be ready for any and all contingencies and the same ethic of military professionalism that has come to characterize the Jordanian commando for the past fifty years, also been the calling card of the Royal Jordanian Air Force (RJAF). The *Al Quwat al Jawwiya al Mlakiya al*

Proudly wearing the national colors on his back, a Royal Jordanian Special Forces free-fallers awaits lift off and flight to 6,000 feet before leaping out over Amman.

Following a 6:30 a.m. briefing, a group of Special Operations Squadron aviators head to their birds for a morning's exercise.

Nearly invisible as they traverse through the desert at Al-Jafr, a squad of Royal Jordanian Special Forces rangers move toward their target during joint training with U.S. Special Forces.

Jump time above Zarqa—a stick of jumpers race out of a "Guts Airline" C-130 during a pre-dawn drop.

Royal Jordanian Special Forces free-fallers glide to earth during early morning jump training in Amman.

His Majesty King Hussein pins the flight wings of the Royal Jordanian Air Force onto a new desert aviator. (Courtesy: RJSOC)

Urduniya, or Royal Jordanian Air Force, was formed on July 22, 1948 at the command of King Abdullah: the air force was small, consisting of nothing larger than a few prop-driven aircraft and only a handful of qualified pilots. For its first fifty years, the main focus of the RJAF was defensive in nature—interceptors defended the national skies. Its armada of fighters and transport aircraft were on call to protect the national frontiers from aggression. The pilots of the interceptor squadrons, the G-suit wearing dog-fighters of the Mirage F-1 and F-5Es, are on-call to meet any breech in the nation's aerial defense's—whether they come from the east, west, south or north. Yet a new offensive spirit has taken hold in the RJAF. It is a special operations spirit made possible by the aerodynamic capabilities of the helicopter, and the skill and courage of the region's finest aviators. It involves flying commandos into harms way, it demands flying by the seat of one's pants, and it demands indescribable courage and infrangible dedication when hovering above a target protected by fusillades of anti-aircraft gunfire. The Special Operations Squadron is such a new equation—and concept—to the RJAF in fact, that the squadron has yet to receive a numeric designation or official emblem. Yet the Special Operations Squadron is a military entity that has harnessed the finest aviators of the RJAF helicopter wing into a cohesive transport force that is designed, by the machines in its armada and the pilots in its rank, to be on call, for missions throughout the country and throughout the region.

Traditionally, the task of transporting the special forces to and from their missions fell to the Airlift Wing, based at the sprawling King Abdullah Air Force Base at Marka, at the northern outskirts of Amman. Established in 1971 with nothing more than a handful of aging C-47 Dakotas from 1 Squadron, and seven Alouette IIIs from 7 Squadron, today the Air Lift Wing consists of several squadrons of C-130 Hercules (known, in the sarcastic humor of the RJAF as "Guts Airline") and CASA 212A Aviocar utility transports, as well as a dozen Aérospatiale AS.332M Super Pumas. Several S.70As are also in use, deployed by the Royal Squadron. The backbone of the wing is 8 Squadron, with its armada of UH-1 choppers. Because of its role in transporting troops and equipment to the outer-reaches of the country, to the farthest desert outpost opposite the Iraqi frontier, to a position near the Syrian border, the Air Lift Wing is one of the busiest units in the RJAF.

The Special Operations Squadron is built around the nucleus of 8 Squadron and its fleet of aging UH-1 workhorses. These Vietnam veterans, all U.S. Army surplus, are surprisingly agile, fast and reliable in the harsh desert conditions of Jordan. "The Hueys are tough and stubborn warriors," claims Major Ahmed, a Special Operations Squadron pilot and senior officer, "even though they are nearly thirty years old, they still show us on a daily basis that they have plenty of kick remaining in them." The UH-1 choppers of the squadron have not been heavily modified since their arrival in Jordan, though their engines have been overhauled. To add some punch to their speed and durability, door-mounted M-60 7.62mm light machine guns provide blankets of supporting cover fire to each chopper. "The Hueys love the desert," claims a warrant officer supervising the maintenance of one of the birds adorned in its darkened olive-drab scheme, "if these aircraft are taken care of, if maintained properly, they have already proven that they can become one with the desert."

The effects of a Royal Jordanian Air Force AH-1 Cobra strike on a series of targets in the desert—seen here during joint-training with the special forces near Zarqa.

A force not to be crossed—a Royal Jordanian Special Forces squad gunner stands for inspection prior to live-fire exercises in the desert.

Pre-operations inspection of a squad heading to a live-fire training area in Zarqa.

Rear-view of the kit carried by a Special Forces radioman.

A Special Forces ranger peers through the sites of his M-16A2 5.56mm assault rifle.

Stoic portrait of a Royal Jordanian Special Forces Ranger rifle platoon.

The best helicopter pilots in the RJAF were offered the opportunity to volunteer into the squadron, and pilots with over 1,000 hours in both the UH-1 and Aérospatiale AS.332M Super Puma, as well as those with over 1,000 hours in the AH-1F Cobra, soon lined up outside the squadron briefing room for an interview. "There is something that we are looking for that goes beyond talent with the throttle or natural flying ability," claims Major Mohammed, a senior officer in the squadron, "and that is personality. In this squadron, a flyer must realize that individual ego and achievement are not as important as the overall success of the mission. There is no room for hot-shots here, no room for top-guns. When we fly in formation, everyone must respect his role, his responsibility, and his importance in the mission at hand. One aberration from perfection in the business that we are in and the special forces miss their LZ, or reach a target detected or not in an ideal position to mount a hostage-rescue assignment." Indeed, the unit is a complex combination of different personalities, and temperaments that blend together to form one very distinctive military formation. In fact, so important was the new unit to the overall scope to Jordanian national defense that His Royal Highness Prince Faisal, the younger brother of His Royal Highness Brigadier Abdullah, an experienced jet fighter pilot, as well as fixed-wing aviator in his own right, was selected to serve as one of the squadron's commanding officers.

A heavy pack under normal circumstances in the field, let alone the 120° (F) in the heat of the Jordanian desert, the operators survive with what they carry on their back.

A Royal Jordanian Special Forces jump instructor readies the thirty-foot training tower for the next candidate.

During live-fire training, a greandier inches closer to advantageous firing position—armed with his M-16A2 5.56mm assault rifle and RPG-7 anti-tank weapon.

The Royal Jordanian Special Force's chief jump instructor explains the do's-and-don'ts of the MC-1C chute.

The Royal Jordanian Special Force's free-fall simulator at King Abdullah Air Force Base in Amman is in constant use by a military force that takes incredible joy and pride in parachuting.

During jump-training, a Royal Jordanian Special Forces jump-instructor watches on as free-fallers pack their square rigs for yet another jump from 4,500 feet.

In the very short time of its operational existence, the Special Operations Squadron has been very busy, indeed. Although the frontiers of Jordan are relatively quiet, the special forces are a very busy unit. Heavily armed smugglers and terrorist operatives routinely infiltrate from the Syrian frontier, and the Iraqi border, a traditional smuggler's route for centuries, has become a battle-zone of sorts between the special forces and heavily armed gun merchants. Fire-fights, some of them truly hellatious, have erupted along the Iraqi border; some have even involved artillery and helicopter gunships. The squadron has, on numerous occasions, come under hostile fire from the smugglers, often flying into the gunsights of multiple barrel anti-aircraft guns, or the IR sensor of a shoulder-launched anti-aircraft missile. For large-scale aerial insertions, the special forces can rely on the Royal Jordanian Air Force's heavy-duty transport choppers, the Aérospatiale AS.332M Super Puma, and for close air support, the commandos rely on the lethal and sleek AH-1F Cobra gunships. It is interesting to note that both the Super Pumas and the Cobras of the RJAF are adorned in a tri-color camouflage schemes while the UH-1s are painted in a dark olive drab pattern. On many missions near the frontier, the Special Operations Squadron have flown with an escort of Cobras—the TOW missiles and 20mm chain gun proving to be an ample deterrent to the smugglers and terrorists attempting to infiltrate into Jordanian territory.

Fighting in areas like the Iraqi frontier, with its unforgiving day-time heat, and night time bone-chilling frost is incredibly difficult for the soldiers to endure and perform in. Desert flying is no simple task, either. Many of the world's most modern combat helicopters fall prey to the heat and dust and flying low in a barren climate that often tops 125° (F) in the

Kukri training with the Royal Jordanian Special Forces.

An icon of power—a Royal Jordanian Special Forces martial arts instructor looks on as his men engage in the indigenous martial arts of Sijal.

shade, and then plummets by eighty degrees to near-freezing frosts. The UH-1, though, has proven up for the task. Much of the flying is done at night, when geographic landmarks disappear and a small mistake in altitude can mean disaster, and the vast emptiness of the desert can fool even the most experienced aviator. Night-vision equipment is worn on many of the night-time operations, but, as one aviator can attest to after returning back to base following a particularly precarious patrol with the special forces, "Night-vision can help, but it is useless unless the pilot knows the terrain, knows his machine, and knows his own capabilities."

There is little down time in the squadron, as the unit finds itself operational—either at the frontiers or in training—virtually seven days a week. At just before dawn, on a windy summer morning, the pilots and air crews of the Special Operations Squadron are assembled in the unit's cool air-conditioned briefing room for the pre-mission briefing. The meeting is conducted with dire seriousness and utter professionalism. After all elements of the mission are explained and examined, the pilots grab their flight bags and head out to their aircraft parked on the sizzling tarmac. After a preflight check, the pilots ready themselves and their birds for the mission—transporting a force of rangers to a sensitive location near the northern frontier. As a RJAF C-130 Hercules comes in for a landing at Marka, one dozen UH-1 slowly lift off in a well-choreographed ascension. The LZ is considered hot and treacherous—several of the choppers must fly into a narrow ravine to unload their cargo of operators, while the remainder of the squadron lands at several kilometers to the east for fire-support. For the Special Operations Squadron, it is just business as usual.

Although the new Middle East, one brought out of a century of conflict by peace accords and common understandings, was supposed to be a safer place, recent terrorist attacks and the rising level of fundamental violence illustrate that the threat to regional security has far

As a proud Brigadier-General Majid Megableh looks on, black-belts and Sijal-experts go through a Taekwondo exercise on the sizzling grounds at Zarqa.

from diminished. If the November 4, 1995 assassination of Israeli Prime Minister Yitzhak Rabin proved anything, it was that peace, no matter how secure, is still a precarious entity in the tumultuous world of the Middle East. In the Hashemite Kingdom of Jordan, as always, it will be the Royal Jordanian Special Forces and the Royal Jordanian Air Force Special Operations Squadron, in the vanguard to not only ensure the prospects of peace, but defeat its enemies, as well.

During exercises with U.S. Special Forces in the desert near Al-Jafr, Royal Jordanian Special Forces and U.S. Special Forces officers greet the commander of the Royal Jordanian Special Operations Command, His Royal Highness Brigadier Abdullah Bin Al-Hussein (center).

During live-fire exercises, a platoon of Royal Jordanian Special Forces rangers line up for inspection.

During joint maneuvers with the U.S. Army 5th Special Forces Group (Airborne), a Royal Jordanian Special Forces radioman calls in a flight of choppers.

SPECIAL OPS

JOURNAL OF THE ELITE FORCES
& SWAT UNITS
VOL.2

GW00567314

CONCORD

PUBLICATIONS COMPANY

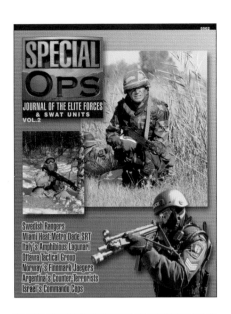

Editor: Samuel M. Katz
Copyright © 1998
by CONCORD PUBLICATIONS CO.
603-609 Castle Peak Road
Kong Nam Industrial Building
10/F, B1, Tsuen Wan
New Territories, Hong Kong

We welcome authors who can help expand our range of books. If you would like to submit material, please feel free to contact us.

We are always on the look-out for new, unpublished photos for this series. If you have photos or slides or information you feel may be useful to future volumes, please send them to us for possible future publication. Full photo credits will be given upon publication.

ISBN 962-361-639-2

printed in Hong Kong

The True Heat In Miami:
The Metro-Dade Police Department's Special Response Team (SRT)
Samuel M. Katz
P 3

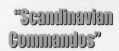

"Scandinavian Commandos"
Elite Units Of The Swedish Defence Forces
Patrik Brandin
P 11

"Canada's Finest"
The Ottawa Police Tactical Group
Gilles Rivet
P 25

Lagunari
The Italian Army's Amphibious Force
Alberto Scarpitta
P 31

Argentina's Cops of Last Resort:
"The State Police Seccion Fuerzas Especiales"
Gilles Rivet
P 42

Norway's Finnmark Jaegers
Yves Debay
P 48

The World's Oldest And Most Volatile Beat!
Special Operations Policing in Israel
Samuel M. Katz
P 52

The True Heat In Miami:
The Metro-Dade Police Department's Special Response Team (SRT)

Samuel M. Katz

During actual assault training, SRT members deploy from a Metro-Dade Aviation Bell-206 Jet Ranger. The Metro-Dade Police Department Patch—regular and subdued at the right upper corner. (Lynn Scrimshaw/Metro-Dade Police Department Media Relations Section)

The team wasn't taking any chances. A ring of snipers and observers, peering through the sights of their scoped M-16A2 5.56mm assault rifles, covered every window of the houseboat in Miami. The South Florida heat was unbearable, though the sharpshooters didn't bother to take their eyes away from their scopes long enough to wipe their brow or grab a drink—the potential for a fire-fight was too great here. The snipers caressed the trigger housings of their weapons with gentle pressure, awaiting the sighting of a threat, and a more dynamic response. The sharpshooters maintained constant communications with the CP, as well as with the officers about to execute a tactical entry on the location. Hundreds of local cops and summoned FBI agents watched closely on an eight-man line of men wearing T-shirts, black utility trousers and wearing black Kevlar Fritz helmets sporting the stencil "SRT." As the eight-men, led by an officer carrying a ballistic shield slinked their way toward the main entrance, a battering ram gained entrance to the location. Flash-bangs were tossed in, and one-by-one the entry team raced into the premises securing room after room until the suspect, a life-less Andrew Cunanan, was found dead with a self-inflicted gun-shot wound to the head.

It was the largest manhunt in recent memory in South Florida—a serial killer on the loose. A cold-blooded killer who had left the dead and destroyed in several states, and had now brought his bloody march to the streets of fashionable Miami Beach with the assassination of famed Italian fashion designer Gianni Versace. Versace, gunned down outside his villa by Andrew Cunanan, was the type of victim that brought an international army of cameramen and news teams to Miami, and guaranteed an intensive law-enforcement effort to apprehend the killer. Faced with a brazen murderer with a propensity for deadly force, Miami and Dade County despatched its super cops to apprehend Cunanan and end his killing spree once and for all.

The incident was just another page in the long and illustrious history of what many in South Florida had known for years—when there is a tactical situation in need of immediate resolution, one where lives are truly on the line, the Metro-Dade Police Department's Special Response Team is the unit that is summoned. And, in recent years, these incidents have been many and varied—from a schoolbus hijacking, to the Valuejet crash, to the murder of Gianni Versace.

The Metro-Dade Police Department is the largest law-enforcement agency in the southeastern United States with 27,000 sworn officers and 1,300 civilian employees providing police services to over 1.9 million residents of South Florida in a geographic region of responsibility covering the 2,139 square miles of Dade County—which includes much of Miami. With the Metro-Dade Police Department also providing security functions to major county facilities such as Miami International Airport, the Port of Miami, and Jackson Memorial Hospital, the department's responsibility for combating the increasing forms of terrorism have increased ten-fold—especially when compared to many other United States municipal police departments and, in terms of their special weapons and tactics units. But Miami, Dade County, is different. In terms of combat, it can be considered a war zone. A homicide is committed every other day, there are twenty felonious incidents reported every hour, and there is more narcotics roaming through the streets of Dade. It is a dangerous place. Since 1980, twenty-seven police officers have been killed in the line of duty. Dozens others have been seriously wounded.

The Metro-Dade Special Response Team (SRT) was formed in 1977 to combat the growing tide of bombings, hijackings and heavy weapons assaults perpetrated on the streets of the county. Originally a "pool" of

Concentrating on both their fast-roping and weapons skills, a two-man SRT tandem engage a window during live-fire training. (Lynn Scrimshaw/Metro-Dade Police Department Media Relations Section)

Utilizing the tactical edge of the "Australian" style of fast-roping, SRT officers engage a target at an open window during assault training exercises near Miami International Airport. (Lynn Scrimshaw/Metro-Dade Police Department Media Relations Section)

tactically trained officers and sergeants assigned to a district's uniform patrol, these specially trained "operators" were assembled from on-duty units as situations necessitated—sometimes, an officer would be pulled off an ongoing arrest or investigation to head to an emergency requiring a tactical response. The officers selected for the "call out" would be based on the individual's specific area of training. This concept, while a stop-gap, was not ideal as it provided poorly assembled and sporadic responses, and on many occasions resulted in an unbalanced team composition. Over the ensuing two decades, a number of changes took place that led to the unit; quickly, however, the unit grew along with Dade County's dizzying growth and development during this time. With that growth and prosperity coupled with the County's proximity to South America, it was inevitable that criminality—especially narco-terrorism—would rise geometrically.

Today, the SRT consists of forty tactical cops divided into five teams—each headed by a sergeant. There are also a dozen hostage-negotiators assigned permanently to the team.

Making police work in Dade County more difficult and far more dangerous is the fact that Miami and its cluster of surrounding areas is a true melting pot of ethnic groups, races and cultures—African Americans, Hispanics, Haitians, displaced Nicaraguans and Hondurans, many of whom have extensive military training. Miami is also the funnel for the national drug trade, and it has made crime in the city and surrounding areas a focal point for the entire United States. The SRT is at

the forefront, and the last line of defense against the most dangerous and most desperate criminal elements. It gets summoned on "call-outs" at least 400 times a year, and since February 1997, has participated in over 500 arrests. Much of SRT's work now is in concert with the elite Narcotics Street Squad (NSS) of the department's Organized Crime Bureau (OCB).

Initially, training consisted of one week focusing on firearms proficiency and chemical agent deployment. Currently, the basic school is three weeks of intensive training with a curriculum including: (a) Firearm qualification (hand gun, shotgun, assault rifle, and automatic weapons); (b) Chemical agents and their deployment; (c) Diversionary devices and their deployment; (d) Rappelling and fast rope insertion skills; (e) Building entries, including the use of explosive entry devices and battering rams; (f) Search techniques; (g) Hostage rescue, including assaulting buildings, automobiles, buses, boats, trains and planes where civilians are being held hostage by either emotionally disturbed people (EDPs), criminals or terrorists; (h) Physical fitness; and, (i) First aid and trauma care to "combat" casualties. It should be noted that SRT instructors frown on classroom time, and instead emphasize on maximum hands on candidate participation.

The Metro-Dade SRT provides services to all but five of the 28 municipalities and numerous state and federal agencies during circumstances which involve potentially life threatening situations. The prime objective of Special Response Teams is the resolution of high-risk

Some of the typical "work tools" deployed by Metro-Dade SRT on the streets of Dade County are displayed here by a five-man element. (Lynn Scrimshaw/Metro-Dade Police Department Media Relations Section)

An SRT officer takes aim with his SIG Sauer 9mm during room entry training in southern Florida. (Lynn Scrimshaw/Metro-Dade Police Department Media Relations Section)

Locked into a stable firing perch by his foot and rope, an SRT officer takes aim with his Heckler and Koch MP5 9mm submachine gun. (Lynn Scrimshaw/Metro-Dade Police Department Media Relations Section)

Great effort is paid to training time at the range—here a five-man team unloads a mixture of 9mm and 12-gauge ammunition at a series of paper targets. (Lynn Scrimshaw/Metro-Dade Police Department Media Relations Section)

Rapid deployment exercises are conducted with a modified 4x4 pick-up turned into an open-air tactics truck. (Lynn Scrimshaw/Metro-Dade Police Department Media Relations Section)

Two officers compare their marksmanship scores and, though nearly perfect, head back to the block for another magazine-emptying burst of proficiency-honing gunfire. (Lynn Scrimshaw/Metro-Dade Police Department Media Relations Section)

police situations with a minimum of force, personal injury, and property damage. The SRT has highly trained supervisors and officers skilled in the use of special weapons, equipment, and techniques designed to reduce the risk to law enforcement personnel and innocent citizens in dangerous situations. "We'd rather talk to someone forever rather than use deadly force," claims an SRT officer removing his gear following a particularly dangerous narcotics warrant near Miami International Airport, "our aim is to get everyone—innocent people, criminals, and EDPs out alive!"

Usually, and the usual rarely holds the line in police work, situations that are likely to require a SRT response, include: (a) Barricaded subjects: including armed felony suspects and mentally unstable individuals; (b) Sniping incidents; (c) Hostage situations and scenarios; (d) Special security risk situations or protection of government officials when such is authorizes, such as providing back-up to the U.S. Secret Service when the President visits, or backing up State Department security when a visiting head of state is in the Dade County area; (e) Search and Arrest Warrants, when considered high-risk (likelihood of armed subjects); (f) Riots, strikes, or civil disorder, to assist Mobile Field Forces (MFF); (g) Hijack Situations, including aircraft, boats, buses, trains and Metro-rail; and, (h) Major aircraft disasters, including those caused by terrorist attack.

The SRT is the most exclusive unit in the Metro-Dade Police Department with a long list of officers from the entire force submitting their requests to volunteer into the squad on a yearly basis. An initial announcement is published throughout the Department to all interested officers with an interest in becoming a member of the Special Response Team and once the applications are received, officers and sergeants are scheduled for a physical test. The test consists of cardio-vascular capacity, strength and a swim test. This must be successfully completed for the candidate to continue in the selection process. After successful completion of a P/T test, an extensive background check is conducted on

Awaiting the deployment of tear-gas during a training exercise, an SRT officer awaits the word to deploy inside a building where "hostages" are being held. (Lynn Scrimshaw/Metro-Dade Police Department Media Relations Section)

An SRT observer peers through his field glasses during a call-out. (Lynn Scrimshaw/Metro-Dade Police Department Media Relations Section)

all candidates. This includes a review of his/her personnel and internal affairs jacket, along with interviews with previous supervisors in the candidates' chain-of-command. If no negative feedback is found, the candidates are administered a psychological exam and an oral interview with a panel of current Special Response Team members to access their capabilities. Preferably, each candidate should have a minimum tenure of five years "on the job." After successful completion of all previous steps, the candidates are placed into the next available three week SRT Basic School. The candidate must complete all aspects of the school curriculum to become certified. They are then placed on a list and selected as vacancies occur.

Because of their tremendous operational activities, SRT members are equipped with a varied catalog of state-of-the-art equipment and gear. The principal SRT weapon is the entire Heckler and Koch MP5 family of 9mm submachine guns in all its variants. SRT members also deploy with the AR-15 5.56mm assault rifle (fitted with different sights and night-scopes) as well as the CAR-15 5.56mm carbine; the Remington M870 Mark 1 U.S. Marine Corps 12-gauge shotgun (many officers favor the sawed off version with an indigenously attached flashlight); M9 Beretta 9mm automatics, and even the old standby, the policeman's favorite, the .38 caliber service revolver; the SIG Sauer 9mm pistol is also becoming a unit staple. Interestingly enough, the Metro-Dade SRT also deploys high-power crossbows in their SRT trucks. Body bunker ballistic shields are carried during most entries, and stun devices are also deployed regularly. A black Kevlar Fritz helmet is worn on all operations, as are

Using a Chevy Caprice squad car as cover, an SRT observer takes aim with his CAR-15 5.56mm assault rifle. (Lynn Scrimshaw/Metro-Dade Police Department Media Relations Section)

In order to flush EDPs, criminals and hostage-takers out of barricaded locations, Metro-Dade SRT will often deploy tear-gas. (Lynn Scrimshaw/Metro-Dade Police Department Media Relations Section)

An SRT officer displays the unit's new camouflaged tac-vests, along with his Remington 870 12-gauge shotgun. (Lynn Scrimshaw/Metro-Dade Police Department Media Relations Section)

fire-proof coveralls (though many officers wear T-shirts in the hot Florida sun), and gas masks are carried in special leg pouches just in case CS agents need to be deployed.

SRT trucks are also tactical tools—not only a means of carrying the gear and bringing the officers to a job. When an entry is hampered by a steel door or gate, a reinforced chain is attached to the rear of the truck and the door and, in the time it takes for the accelerator pedal being pushed down, the steel gate or door flung open like a beer can being popped. SRT also deploys Zodiac craft and speedboats for seaborne and even underwater tactical assignments. Trained by the U.S. Navy SEALs and Special Forces divers, SRT personnel are trained and equipped to end a hostage situation in mid-water, by reaching a boat or craft through SCUBA underwater, and not having the bad guys know that they've deployed until the words "FREEZE: POLICE" are heard. Metro-Dade Aviation Unit Bell-206L4 Jet Ranger choppers also support many SRT operations, and these choppers have recently been equipped with FLIR (Forward Looking Infra-Red) capabilities for night time assaults and chases.

Clearly, the "job" that brought the SRT the most attention was the November 2, 1995 hijacking of a schoolbus loaded with handicapped children in Miami Beach by one Nick Sang, a man with a grudge against the Internal Revenue Service. It was early in the morning and the bus and thirteen children were en route to the Blue Lakes Elementary School when Sang boarded the bus, said he was armed with a gun and a bomb,

At a Dade County housing project, an SRT officer displays the unit's ballistic bunker body shield—used on virtually all entries. (Lynn Scrimshaw/Metro-Dade Police Department Media Relations Section)

and ordered the driver to proceed toward the sea front tourist area. Police soon gave chase and, in an eerie scene reminiscent of the O.J. Simpson Bronco chase and a clip from the Hollywood film "Speed" the embattled schoolbus was seen on a slow and deliberate path to "wherever" it was going followed by a small flotilla of white and green Metro-Dade Police Department radio cars, along with an equal number of Florida State Troopers and Highway Patrol cars. The parents of the children watched the ongoing events in absolute horror, and the police were equally daunted. "What if the psycho really has a bomb?" police supervisors were heard uttering to one another over a secured frequency. This was the absolute nightmare scenario and nobody wanted it to go down on their watch.

When the hijacking commenced, the SRT was involved in an early morning training session involving storming fortified crack houses. Although the squad had performed that dangerous task thousands of times FOR REAL, the skills were honed on the training field on a weekly basis. The moment the first "911" came over the radio, the officers stopped in their tracks and paused for a brief moment—if this was fake it was a sick joke; if it was for real then they'd be heading for Miami Beach in a matter of moments. Five minutes later, the entire SRT was called up and racing for Miami's scenic beach waterfront.

Police followed the bus' movements and plotted a course where it would possibly travel to; the driver, a brave middle-aged woman, had been acting as liaison between the hijacker and police with a cellular phone, informed them that he was heading toward "Joe's Stone Crab," a famed Miami sidewalk restaurant. The SRT established an inner perimeter, snipers were positioned and the face-off waited for. When the bus arrived, police vehicles cordoned it off and a brief—very brief—stand-off ensued. When police officials feared that the hijacker would make good on his threats and kill a hostage or blow up the bus with the bomb he said was in his possession, the SRT was ordered to move in. Two

Prior to raiding a Miami crack-house, SRT officers are briefed at a field tac-meeting. (Lynn Scrimshaw/Metro-Dade Police Department Media Relations Section)

During an actual hostage-taking incident at a Miami pizza parlor, a five-man SRT team moves in toward firing position. (Lynn Scrimshaw/Metro-Dade Police Department Media Relations Section)

During a call-out when tear-gas will be deployed, a two-man entry tandem assist one another with the affixing of their protective gas masks. (Lynn Scrimshaw/Metro-Dade Police Department Media Relations Section)

Following the successful execution of a warrant, a five-man element is driven back to their home-base near Miami International Airport. (Lynn Scrimshaw/Metro-Dade Police Department Media Relations Section)

snipers fired simultaneous 7.62mm rounds from their Heckler and Koch PSG-1 7.62mm sniper rifles, mortally wounding Sang. Almost simultaneously, a SRT fire-team moved in to remove the badly bleeding hijacker, while a second team moved in at the same time to rescue the bewildered children. As police kept a watch on Sang, as he lay dying on a Miami sidewalk, the Metro-Dade Police Department Bomb-Squad searched the bus for explosives. None were found.

SRT officers high-fived one another at the scene—relieved beyond the expression of words that all the children had been saved. "There is no greater joy than when you can save the life of a helpless child," claimed one of the snipers. It was clear that beyond the skills and abilities of the SRT was the fact that the city and the police department had enough faith in the unit and confidence in their abilities to deploy them in such a precarious scenario.

There is only so much that the SRT can do—a fact not lost to political and police officials in Florida. In 1994, Florida Governor Bob Graham and other state officials concerned about the vulnerability of Florida's busy airports, seaports and tourist attractions (like Disney World) to terrorist attack considered a proposal to develop a statewide anti-terrorist squad within the Florida Department of Law Enforcement (FDLE). According to Graham, as quoted by the Fort-Lauderdale Sun-Sentinel, "We know on a daily basis our territory is invaded by small

Following the Valuejet crash, SRT officers assisted the rescuers and recovery experts by covering their search of the Florida Everglades with CAR-15 fire to dissuade any alligator from making a threatening move. (Lynn Scrimshaw/Metro-Dade Police Department Media Relations Section)

The chaos and the terror of that initial entry: SRT officers race through the front door of a Miami crack house ready for anything they might encounter—from a pitbull to a ten-year-old cradling a shotgun. (Metro-Dade Police Department/SRT)

One of the unit's premier precision weapons—the M-16 5.56mm assault rifle. SRT marksman also uses the Remington M-24 system. (Metro-Dade Police Department/SRT)

SRT officers examine weapons seized inside a crack-house. (Metro-Dade Police Department/SRT)

9

planes and boats bringing drugs and refugees. Those same planes and boats could bring terrorists and bombs. We have a special stake in being prepared." The understood threat in Florida is not from Arabs, such as in the bombing of the World Trade Center or the Jewish Center in Buenos Aires, but from various Latin American and South American countries with unstable political situations. Under the proposed plan, the FDLE anti-terrorist squad would not solely be a counter-terrorist squad, but would also work hand-in-hand with other municipal and county SWAT units and police agencies in the execution of high-risk assignments (such as major arrests at drug stash houses and statewide manhunts for dangerous fugitives). The planned FDLE unit would be trained and supported by the FBI HRT.

The SRT, it should be mentioned, has trained side-by-side with the FBI's HRT, the U.S. Secret Service, the Ohio State Police, the FDLE, and U.S. Army and U.S. Navy counter-terrorist units. The SRT has also trained foreign counter-terrorist units, including elements from the Royal Moroccan Intelligence Service, the Portuguese national police, and the Panamanian police, as well. Memorabilia from all these cross-training contacts decorate the unit's Spartan headquarters at the Midwest Police Station near Miami International Airport. When not on regular patrol duties, responding to 911 calls and issuing summonses, the "SRT Room" is a nerve-center from where the unit turns out from and responds to emergencies. No one can ever predict when the call will come, but as the large arsenal of weaponry in the room's armory indicates, and the unit's fleet of specialized vehicles prove, SRT is ready for any and all emergencies!

Personal and protective equipment worn by SRT officers on entries and tactical deployments. (Metro-Dade Police Department/SRT)

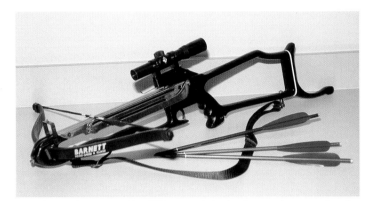

A crossbow, used by SRT on certain deployments, as well as for the silent removal of pitbulls and Rottweilers often used by drug dealers. (Metro-Dade Police Department/SRT)

The most precarious moments of a "hit"—going through the mysteries and dangers of "what's behind the door." (Metro-Dade Police Department/SRT)

Gas grenades and tactical diversionary devices used by SRT. (Metro-Dade Police Department/SRT)

Poled-mirrors and other entry devices used by SRT. (Metro-Dade Police Department/SRT)

10

"Scandinavian Commandos"
Elite Units Of The Swedish Defence Forces

Patrik Brandin

Infiltration during a Ranger exercise in northern Sweden.

For a nation known throughout the world for its neutrality, high-standard of living and liberal policies on human rights, Sweden has, for centuries, safeguarded its freedoms by maintaining a highly aggressive, and completely independently-minded, system of national defense that relied on Swedish industry for advanced weapons systems, and Swedish citizens for conscripted military service. When all of Europe went to war in 1914 and again in 1939, Sweden maintained its territorial integrity undaunted by pressures from both the Allies and the Axis powers. And, when Europe was gripped by the Cold War, pitting the Warsaw Pact against NATO, Sweden once again found itself as anxious observers to a continent determined to stand at the brink. Today, as a New World Order has redefined old boundaries and traditional political allegiances, Sweden continues to march to the beat of its own drum and maintain a defense force considered among the most capable in Europe with a highly-integrated and vast network of special operations units who are not only expert assault commandos and counter-terrorist operators, but also considered among the world's premier cold-weather fighting forces.

The Swedish Defence is built on a conscript Army. Most of the officer corps are regulars. The basic training last from seven to fifteen months depending on the specific military occupation (MOS). During every one year period, approximately 24,000 men are called up for basic training into either the Army, Air Force and Naval Forces (Coastal Artillery and Navy). After completing basic training the soldiers are war-posted and put in the reserve, with occasional call-ups that guarantee unit

AUTHOR PHOTO. Born in February 1969, Patrik Brandin served as a Ranger squad leader at Northland Dragoon Regiment, eventually reaching the rank of sergeant. He has participated in peacekeeping missions in Macedonia, Lebanon and Bosnia and currently works in the security field in Gothenburg, Sweden.

Like other western airborne troops the Swedish Parachute Rangers wear the maroon beret.

A Parachute Ranger squad infiltrating an area with round parachutes during a guerrilla warfare exercise.

readiness in time of war—even though Sweden has not fought a war since 1814. Nevertheless, thousands of Swedish soldiers have served with UN peace-keeping forces around the world, including: Cyprus, Lebanon, Somalia and Bosnia.

A small cadre of conscripts each year volunteer to endure among the world's toughest military training regimens. Among the largest "elite units" within the Swedish defense forces are the Rangers, which in Sweden are known simply as *Jägare*. There are five different regiments in Sweden which trains Ranger units. Army Parachute Ranger School (FJS) trains Parachute Rangers (*Fallskärmsjägare*), Vaxholms Coast Artillery Regiment (KA1) trains Coastal Rangers and Attack Divers (*Kustjägare* and *Attackdykare*), Northland Dragoon Regiment (K4) trains the Northland Rangers (*Norrlandsjägare*), Life Hussar Regiment (K3)

trains the "regular" Rangers (*Jägare*), and Lapland Ranger Regiment (I22) trains the Lapland Rangers (*Lapplandsjägare*).

ARMY PARACHUTE RANGER SCHOOL (FJS)

The Swedish Army Parachute Ranger School (situated in Karlsborg) was formed in 1952 after the British model. To get the necessary knowledge some Swedish officers were sent to Great Britain and the United States for advanced airborne and parachuting instruction at Brize Norton RAF and Fort Benning. The main mission for the Para-Rangers are intelligence gathering and sabotage deep behind enemy lines for long periods without support from friendly forces. The Para-Rangers are organized into five-man patrols consisting of an officer in command, a deputy patrol commander/signaler, a sniper armed with a PSG-90 7.62mm (Accuracy International) or an AG-90 12.7mm (Barrett long

The drop zone for Parachute Ranger are usually frozen lakes or rivers.

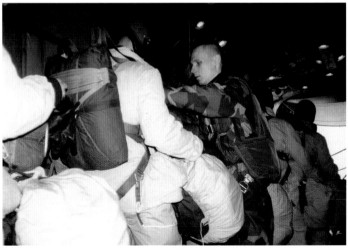

Last check by the jump master inside the C-130 before a jump during a winter exercise.

The Parachute Ranger qualification badge — the Golden Eagle is worn on the left breast pocket of the service dress and a subdued patch on the combat uniform.

Fallskärmsjägarna *combat surface swimming after a jump from a combat boat.*

A Fallskärmsjägare *dressed in a dry suit and ready for a "wet jump.*

From well hidden observation post Parachute Rangers observe enemy movement during guerrilla-warfare exercises.

range sniper rifle), a demolition expert and a medic. The equipment on the patrol are different depending on their specific mission.

Parachute Ranger training last fifteen months. The selection process for ranger-hopefuls is tough and demanding, arduous and highly competitive. Each year, approximately 600 volunteer but less than half pass the initial selection examinations that consists of harsh physical and mental exercises. Eventually, only 100 are selected for the Parachute Ranger course. The Parachute Ranger course starts each and every June with instruction in basic military skills and basic jump-school training, following the first jump from a Swedish Air Force C-130 Hercules the Parachute Ranger hopeful is issued with the coveted maroon beret. Following four month of basic military training, the Rangers are put through what is referred to as the "Eagle March." Beginning with a parachute jump into the dense forests of central Sweden, the soldiers must march seventy-kilometers with nearly twenty-five kilograms on their back within a twenty-four-hour time-frame. Every few kilometers or so, the soldiers must perform a varied array of tasks, ranging from a close-quarter combat course to basic survival tests, and they must not stray from the time-frame of their one day limit. Many ranger-hopefuls do not make it out of "Eagle March"—some need to be rescued from the thick wooded areas. Those who negotiate the course successfully, however, receive the coveted "Parachute Ranger Qualification Badge" and are one step closer in being fully accepted into the unit. The course continues with different combat and airborne training—nearly forty jumps are carried out over the course of the instruction—from both round and square rigs.

From December to March, the course moves north up to the Lapland Ranger Regiment for Arctic training. After that the course continues with combat surface swimming, wet jumps and helo-casting in the archipelago of Stockholm. The final test is a three-week long field exercise where all the skills are performed. Of the 100 that initially started out on the course, only a handful survive the ten months of back-breaking and mind-numbing experience. Those who pass can eventually, and proudly, proclaim the words: *"The will to do, the courage to do it and the endurance to see it through"*—the motto of Parachute Rangers.

The weaponry used in the Parachute Ranger patrol are the AK5 5.56mm assault rifle (the indigenous and improved variant of the FNC), AK5B with scope, AK5C with M203 40mm grenade launcher, KSP-90 5.56mm (FN Minimi LMG) and various heavy weapons and mines depending on the mission.

COASTAL RANGERS (KJ)

The Swedish Coastal Artillery trains Amphibious Battalions equipped with heavy firepower—their responsibility is combat operations in the archipelago of Sweden. The battalion consist of a HQ company, a mortar company, an amphibious company which includes anti-boat missile and mine-laying units, and two Coastal Ranger companies. The Coastal Ranger company's prime mission is to retake territory that the enemy has seized—primarily the beachhead captured during an amphibious assault. Other missions like reconnaissance and anti-sabotage missions are also given to the Coastal Rangers.

The unit consists of three ranger platoons divided in three squads and two support sections armed with KSP-58 7.62mm (FN MAG) and 84mm Carl Gustav recoilless rifles. Coastal Ranger squads are armed with AK5, AK5B, AK5C, and the KSP-90. To move about fast in the icy waters of the Swedish coast, the Coastal Rangers use a wide assortment of fast craft, including rubber inflatables, high-speed squad support vessels and, always at the ready, the Navy's fleet of transport helicopters. For covert operations Coastal Rangers use Klepper kayaks for silent insertion.

Like the Parachute Rangers, the selection process for volunteers hoping to serve in a Coastal Ranger unit is rough. Volunteers are examined on their mental and physical strengths, as well as their determination. Coastal Ranger training lasts ten months and takes place at Vaxholm and in the archipelago of Stockholm. After the first six months of training, Coastal Ranger candidates are put through a Ranger march, it will push soldiers to the envelope of his endurance. The tests are carried out in a span of a week, and consists of a series of forced marches similar to the "Eagle March" with the Parachute Rangers. Many do not survive the week, though all those passing earn the right to wear the commando green beret and the Coastal Ranger qualification badge for the Coastal Rangers-Neptune's Trident. During the remainder of their basic combat and assault training, Coastal Rangers receive additional instruction on long distance kayak paddling, maritime obstacle courses, speed marches, demolitions, navigation, close-quarter killing, and urban assault courses.

Coastal Rangers during an obstacle course. Notice the ice blocks on the surface. The obstacle course is done in full combat gear.

Covered with mud these Coastal Rangers are put through a tough obstacle course during physical training.

A Coastal Ranger support section armed with 84mm Carl Gustav recoilless rifle and AK5 5.56mm assault rifles.

A well armed Kustjägare equipped with AK5C (with 40mm M203 grenade launcher), wearing the commando green beret with Neptune trident.

14

Nearly invisible in the woodland backdrop, a Coastal Ranger sharpshooter taking aim with his AK5B accurized sniper rifle.

The Klepper kayaks, capable of carrying two operators and their equipment, is among the most successful means of infiltration used by the Coastal Rangers and Attack Divers.

Coastal Rangers disembark from an assault boat during a beach assault exercise.

A Coastal Ranger on a reconnaissance mission, observing the enemy movement on an island outside Stockholm during a field exercise.

A Coastal Ranger Sergeant from the 4th Amphibious Battalion displays the commando green beret with Neptune trident as a beret badge.

Coastal Rangers inside a Mk.90 combat boat prior to an assault, poised to capture enemy territory, during mock assault training.

THE ATTACK DIVERS

Attack Divers, attached to the unit's reconnaissance platoon, are tasked with, perhaps the most difficult of tasks in naval special warfare—landing onto an enemy position before a larger-scale amphibious assault and act as command's eyes and ears on ground zero. The Recon platoon belongs to the HQ company but the Attack Divers are recruited from Coastal Rangers. The Attack Divers' missions include: intelligence-gathering and other special reconnaissance, sabotage and lightning raids, calling in mortar and artillery fire, and serving as spearheads for attacking forces of landing crafts. To achieve their mission, Attack Divers are ferried to objectives by rubber inflatables, speed boats, Kleppers, and Swedish Navy helicopters. And, of course, their combat-swimming skills are the ultimate in stealth-like infiltration methods. Attack Divers deploy both open and closed circuit diving systems, though closed-circuit systems are favored for underwater infiltration.

The Attack Divers belong to the Recon platoon in the HQ company, each divided into three squads with six Attack Divers in each squad. Every diver has a specific occupation: commander, deputy commander, sniper, navigator/boat handler, demolition expert and signaler. They are armed with AK5 5.56mm assault rifle (FNC), AK5B (with scope), AK5C (with M-203 40mm grenade launcher), AK5 with laser pointer and KSP-90 5.56mm (FN Minimi LMG). The squad is well equipped for night fighting, and is trained to operate with a full-array of infra-red and other night-fighting devices. Attack Divers are recruited from the already elite Coastal Ranger company after a selection test. Their training lasts ten months and teaches the soldiers diving with open and closed systems, combat survival, small unit tactics, hand-to-hand combat, sabotage and more special operation skills.

Attack Divers are put through the same combat training as Coastal Rangers and also wear the Commando green beret and Neptune's Trident but with tines bent inwards. Attack Divers also wear the Swedish Defense diver qualification badge.

Training tactical submersion in the pool at KA1 in Vaxholm. Tactical submersion is perfected in the pool before the real thing using weapons for drill purpose. Attack Divers always work in pairs. The road to becoming an Attack Diver is a long and arduous one, requiring an individual's discipline, motivation and 110 percent.

Attack Divers ready for an infiltration exercise. The boat is a speed boat issued to all squads. The Divers are dressed in dry suits and wearing combat uniform underneath.

Attack Diver wearing dry suits and AGA oxydive closed circuit breathing apparatus preparing to come ashore for a sabotage mission. He is armed with a KSP-90 5.56mm (FN Minimi LMG) ready to lay down covering fire for his partner already on shore.

Two Attack Divers taking up position with their weapons during an infiltration exercise.

Attack Divers planning for a reconnaissance mission, they are armed with AK5, AK5C and AK5B. Notice the Attack Divers qualification patches on the right arm.

Going through a combat and survival exercise, operators learn to survive in hostile territory cut-off from their regular methods of resupply. Attack Divers learn to cook wild animals and other sources of protein milling about the wilderness, and they are trained to eat plants and insects, as well.

A good view of the commando green beret with Neptune trident with inbent tines indicating he is an Attack Diver.

The insertion of an Attack Diver squad is done by submarine, helicopter, speedboats or kayaks.

An Attack Diver showing his qualification patches: Coastal Rangers Neptune trident, Swedish Defence diver qualification patch are worn on the right arm of the combat uniform.

Attack Divers are about to explore an enemy taken island to provide the Amphibious Battalion commander with information about the enemy's deployment.

Attack Divers are transported in a squad boat between different islands during a field exercise.

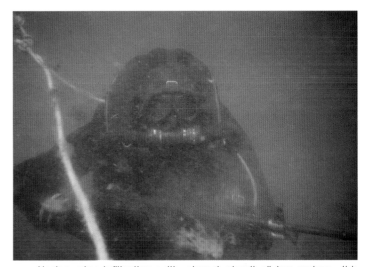

Underwater infiltration with closed circuit diving system, this Attack Diver is armed with a KSP-90 5.56mm.

Attack Divers are captured and searched during an escape and evasion exercise. The Hunter Force consists of former Rangers and policemen with trained tracker dogs.

An Attack Diver squad consists of six specialists: commander, deputy commander, sniper, navigator/boat handler, demolition expert and a signaller.

Securing the beach before coming ashore, two Attack Divers ready for anything!

Armed with an AK5 5.56mm with a folding stock, this Attack Diver scans the hostile surroundings for enemy activity, ready to open fire.

An Attack Diver during a reconnaissance exercise somewhere on the islands of Sweden dressed in rain-proof clothing.

NORTHLAND RANGERS (K4)

The Northland Dragoon Regiment (K4) is located at Arvidsjaur in the northern region of Sweden, and is one of the oldest regiments in the Swedish military, originating around the 17th-Century. At that time, the Regiment trained Dragoons on horses which is why they still possess the designation as a cavalry unit. In the mid-1970s, when the focus of military moved to the special forces arena, the unit began to train as rangers. The Regiment is responsible for training independent Arctic Ranger battalions. Their tasks are reconnaissance and combat missions in the enemies rear areas—primarily consisting of long-range ambushes with wire-guided anti-tank missiles, mortars, snipers and land-mines. A Northland Ranger battalion consists of 500 operators trained and cross-trained at different military tasks. The prime combat unit are the six-man Ranger squad with a squad leader, deputy squad leader/signaler, two heavy weapon experts, demolition expert and a medic. Snipers can be assigned depending on the mission. The squads weaponry are the same as the other Ranger units, with heavy weaponry including the Carl Gustav 84mm recoilless rifle, and 84mm AT-4 rocket launcher. The mortar section uses 80mm mortars. Mines are a vital part in Ranger warfare. Most of the equipment is carried in backpacks and during winter dragged in sleds, scooters, bandwagons (over snow vehicle) and four-wheel all terrain vehicles.

The Northland Ranger training are aimed at knowledge of the enemy, Ranger special combat techniques and survival in hostile surroundings. The mark of a qualified Northland Ranger is the green beret with a golden ND badge and a black/yellow Ranger tab inspired by U.S. Army Ranger School tab.

A Northland Ranger wearing the green Ranger beret with the golden ND badge and the black and yellow Ranger tab on the left arm identifying him as a fully trained Ranger.

Mines are a vital part in the Swedish Ranger warfare. A Ranger places a No.14 anti-vehicle mine into position before an ambush during a field maneuver.

Terrain is no obstacle for a Northland Ranger, the mission must be completed. Cliff and rock climbing are practiced, a Ranger from K4 rappelling down a cliff wearing backpack and personal weapon.

A Northland Ranger platoon with heavy backpacks moves in file across the snow covered terrain of the northern parts of Sweden.

A Northland Ranger ready to rappelling down a cliff wearing M/90 camouflage uniform and the old standard weapon of the Swedish Army—the AK4 7.62mm (G3).

RANGERS (K3)

The Life Hussar Regiment (K3) is an old cavalry unit, like K4 from the 17th-Century, that specialized in cavalry training. In the mid-1950s, the Regiment began to train reconnaissance units and, in 1975, became ranger-qualified tasked with operations in central and southern Sweden. The Ranger battalion's prime task is reconnaissance and combat operations behind the enemy lines—identical in equipment and tasks to the Northland Ranger battalions. The unit is designed to function, unhindered, in all types of terrain and conditions, ranging from dense forests in the summer to blizzards and Arctic-like conditions in the winter. Ranger training is hard and demands physically and mentally fit soldiers. The course is divided in three phases. "Phase 1" consists of basic Military and Ranger skills. The would-be Rangers are taught weapon handling, patrolling, survival, map and compass reading, and other basic combat skills. During "Phase 2," the soldiers are taught a specific patrol skill, ranging from sharp-shooting to tank-killing. "Phase 3" is devoted to training the squad and platoon for full-fledged combat operations.

Like all the other Ranger units the K3 Ranger wears a green beret with three crowns as a badge. A green/black Ranger tab is worn on the left shoulder.

Rangers from Life Hussar Regiment rappel from a UH-1 helicopter during an infiltration exercise.

This Swedish Ranger uses the AT-4 anti-tank rocket launcher against a convoy of approaching enemy APCs.

A Ranger sniper team giving fire during ambush drills. The sniper is armed with PSG-90 7.62mm (Accuracy International).

To blend in the bush surroundings, snipers use Ghillie suits. You can stand on them without noticing them. Ranger snipers can operate in a squad or independently depending on the mission.

Seen through night vision goggles, this Ranger's weapon is an AK5B with a night vision device. Ranger units are well equipped with night vision capacity.

Sniping is an important part of a Ranger operation. This sniper is dressed in a Ghillie suit for maximum camouflage and is armed with a PSG-90 7.62mm sniper rifle (Accuracy International).

Heavily armed terrain vehicle issued to the anti-tank missile platoons at K3. It carries a RBS-56 BILL anti-tank missile launcher, KSP-58 7.62mm (FN MAG), AT-4 anti-tank rocket launchers, 84mm Carl Gustav recoilless rifle and other equipment.

LAPLAND RANGERS (I22)

The Lapland Ranger Regiment was created in 1945, when it was known as the Army Ranger School, but in 1975 was upgraded to a fully functional Regiment. Every year I22 trains 350 Rangers who, upon completion of the year-long training, is posted to the ultra-strategic north of Sweden. The Lapland Ranger Regiment trains independent Ranger companies to perform behind-enemy-lines communications disruption in the often desolate terrain of Sweden's northern frontier (the highlight of the Lapland course requires each and every ranger-hopeful to climb to the summit of Mt. Kebenekaise, Sweden's highest mountain which reaches 2,117 meters above sea-level). The 100-man strong Ranger company consists of a HQ squad, two Ranger platoons, mortar section and an anti-tank missile platoon. A Ranger platoon consists of four squads, with eight rangers in each. The Ranger squad consists of two squad leaders, one sniper team, one heavy weapons team, a medic, signaler and all-terrain vehicle drivers. The weaponry deployed is the same as the others elite units in the Swedish military though the unit is particularly efficient in its deployment of the RBS-56 BILL anti-tank missile system.

The helicopter is used for re-supply, medevac and transportation for recon missions.

The heavy backpack contains necessary equipment to support the Ranger for a long period of time that will be spent behind enemy lines. The backpack usually weights about thirty-five kilograms and contains a stove, sleeping bag, food, extra clothing, one-man tent, rain clothing and additional supplies of ammunition.

A Lapland Ranger support section giving fire with their KSP-58 7.62mm (FN MAG) during ambush training.

Lapland Rangers going through a combat survival exercise during winter times.

To cross rivers or lakes Rangers are issued a two-man patrol boat in each squad.

Learning to handle foreign weapons like the AKM are one of the skills taught to Swedish Ranger units.

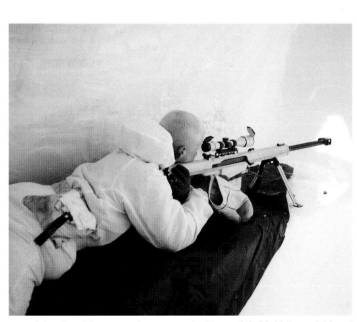

A Lapland Ranger sniper armed with an AG-90 12.7mm (.50 cal Barrett) taking aim at selected targets from a concealed position.

Ranger sniper wearing Arctic clothing and a white face mask for protection against the cold and for the obvious camouflage benefits. His sniper rifle PSG-90 7.62mm is covered with white cloth and tape.

To qualify for the combat survival patch Rangers go through a SERE (Survival, Escape, Resistance, Evasion) exercise which ends with being captured and interrogated after being hunted by an "enemy" force.

Ranger winter survival training includes scenarios such as an operator falling through the ice and the means required to save his life.

Close-up view of two Lapland Rangers with their weapons AK5 and AT-4 84mm rocket launcher, M/90 camouflage uniforms, backpacks and field caps, the right headgear to wear during maneuvers.

The wolf's head is the symbol of a Lapland Ranger, and is worn on the green beret and as a shoulder patch on the left side of the combat uniform.

"Canada's Finest"
The Ottawa Police Tactical Group

Gilles Rivet

Operators from the Tactical Group pose for the camera following the successful completion of a day of training.

When one thinks of Canada, especially the capital city Ottawa, the images of urban blight and high-crime do not come to mind. And, while Canada's law enforcement agencies have done a remarkable job in keeping crime relatively low throughout the provinces, the nation's streets are not crime free, and the dangers posed by criminals, armed psychos, and the narcotics trade are encountered on a daily basis. The image of heavily armed SWAT-cops, bursting through a door with a battering ram, and arresting a multitude of suspects was once thought of as an exclusively American domain, yet that reality is becoming more and more an element of the Canadian national landscape. From the picturesque splendor of Vancouver and British Colombia, to the urban steel of Toronto, to the attempts to replicate a North American vision of France in Quebec, the matter of crime in Canada has resulted in local agencies taking on a more aggressive and innovative role in keeping its citizens safe. That reality is also part and parcel of the daily life in Ottawa, the national capital.

Although by American standards—even those in some major European cities—crime in Ottawa is relatively low, the local catchword has always been "It is better to warn than to heal!" Being prepared and ready rather than having to respond ill-equipped has always been the preferred method of handling all matters of law enforcement in the national capital, and it has been a very successful professional ethic applied to everything from littering to burglaries. That approach has also

A Tactical Group sniper peers through the sights of his M-16A2 5.56mm assault rifle. Other snipers in the unit are also equipped with the Remington M-24 system.

25

One of the most difficult aspects of tubular assaults is the explosive seconds entry when the barrier separating cops from the perpetrators (and potentially, the hostages) is breached. As a result, any "opening" must be viewed as a potential entry point—especially windows. Here, at the unit's training grounds, various entry tactics employing rappelling and rope skills are perfected.

been most successful in the arena of police tactical operations. In 1976, however, only four years following the Munich Olympic Massacre, the Ottawa-Carleton Regional Police Service, protecting and serving the residents of Gloucester, Nepean, Ottawa and Vanier, formed the "Tactical Group." Today, they are considered Canada's Finest.

The Ottawa-Carleton Regional Police Service (OCRPS) is not a large force by most major metropolitan standards—with just under 1,000

The assault element of an intervention team receives their entry instructions from the "team chief" during exercises. They are armed with SIG P226 9mm handgun, and the Heckler and Koch MP5A3 9mm submachine gun.

officers, it is responsible for a large stretch of territory and nearly one million inhabitants. And, as a result, from its creation in 1976 to 1993, officers serving in the Tactical Group did so on a part-time and mission-demanding basis. Operators on the team worked their regular shifts, be it as a traffic cop or homicide detective, and trained sparingly throughout the week, or even on their own time, in the art of police special operations and tactics. In 1993, however, the unit became a full-time, 100% professional, entity. Officers serving in the unit no longer juggled their busy schedule in order to be able to attend a tubular-assault exercise, or spend additional hours on the range. Instead, the Tactical Group looked to SWAT units in the United States (and, indeed, even several notable teams in Canada) to create an on-call force ready to respond, at a moment's notice, to any tactical assignment the regular patrol force could not handle. To maximize their abilities and response time to protect the community and provide tactical back-up to the patrol force in the field, two-men Tactical Group tandems patrol the city streets ready to be first responders to any potential crisis.

RECRUITMENT AND FORMATION

There are thirty-four officers in the Ottawa-Carleton Regional Police Service Tactical Group, including one female officer. An exclusively volunteer force, the Tactical Group only accepts "wanna-be's" with an exemplary service record and a minimum of four-years on the job. A Tactical Group volunteer must undergo exhaustive psycho-technical and psychological examinations, score high marks on a grueling physical test, and pass a series of interviews designed to determine the officer's determination, motive and desires in attempting to become a member of the elite of the Ottawa-Carleton Regional Police Service. The attrition rate for the selection process is very high, and officers who do not make

Once inside a target, the advance needs to be swift, careful, and unabated. Here, Tactical Group operators gingerly head up a stair-case toward a series of paper-targets.

the cut simply return to the force—no black marks held against them.

Once admitted into the unit, the new element-member commences his advanced tactical instruction by teaming up with an experienced member of the group, and attending the various classes provided to the team on a bi-weekly basis when a particular group of officers are neither on patrol or on stand-by status. Points of instruction include:

- Precision shooting
- Tubular assaults (trains, buses, buildings)
- Rural operations (a large part of the Ottawa-Carleton Regional Police Service area consists of suburbs and even farm-land)
- Handling of barricaded suspects and EDPs (emotionally disturbed persons)

Recently, the Ottawa-Carleton Regional Police Service Tactical Group has assumed responsibility for operations area airports—more specifically, the Tactical Group is responsible for operations and potential hostage-rescue should a "domestic" carrier is hijacked. An international aircraft diverted to Ottawa would become the responsibility of the Canadian Army's Joint Task Force-Two (JTF-2), the national hostage-rescue force; a force, according to reports, also based in Ottawa. Aircraft rescues are one of the most difficult aspects of the science known as "tubular assaults," and Tactical Group officers train with elements from a myriad of domestic and foreign agencies—from JTF-2 and the Royal Canadian Mounted Police, to units and departments in the United States and Europe—to hone and perfect their skills, tactics, and abilities. Such training is involved, demanding, diverse, and expensive. As a result, the commanders of the Ottawa-Carleton Regional Police Service have seen to it that the Tactical Group is lavishly funded.

A piece of hardware considered irreplaceable in virtually all of the world's tactical police formations—the Heckler and Koch MP5 9mm submachine—seen here in the hands of a Tactical Group "chief" during assault exercises.

A Tactical Group entry team lines up for the entry and assault. Note Glico 9mm handgun equipped with flashlight attachment.

Executing an entry, while under fire, is perhaps one of the most dangerous aspects of police special operations. A Tactical Group entry team pauses for cover, before they deploy a ladder to a second-story window during building-assault exercises.

Just as important as a SWAT cop's MP5, handgun or Body Bunker, are his entry devices. Here, Tactical Group operators deploy a Hooligan (also known as Halogen) tool prior to reaching the targeted door.

Explosive photograph of a training exercise where the officers endure changing situations during what was supposed to be routine training. Initially tasked with entering a location through a second story window, Tactical Group officers respond to shots fired inside the location by smashing through a first-floor window.

ORGANIZATION OF THE TACTICAL GROUP

A Police Master Sergeant commands the thirty-four strong Tactical Group, with the four eight-officer teams, each commanded by a sergeant (known in the unit vernacular as a "team chief"); the unit also possesses an adjutant-sergeant, and a training sergeant. Each operational team also maintains two snipers. Each team, by itself, is trained to function as an independent element, though many of the unit's warrants and call-outs are handled by several teams; sometimes, even, the entire unit. The unit works on a rotating shift schedule, affording teams the opportunity to train while others are patrolling the region's streets.

The Tactical Group operates in a fleet of ten 4x4 vehicles—the cars are driven by steady two-man partners, who carry all their equipment with them in the vehicle's storage area. The gear includes: tactical vests, ammunition, gas masks, Kevlar helmet, rope and rappelling gear, diversionary devices and smoke grenades. Weaponry carried by each two-man tandem includes: two Heckler and Koch MP5 9mm submachine guns, one M-16 5.56mm assault rifle, two 9mm automatics, and one .357 magnum revolver. Specialized equipment includes one .308 Remington sniper rifle and supporting gear, as well as a 37mm tear-gas launcher.

A Tactical Group team poses for the camera, displaying the unit's compliment of MP5s, Benelli 12-gauge shotguns, and M-16A2 5.56mm assault rifles.

"Showtime in Ottawa!" A team element leader moves about in front of his seven-officer support crew, his fingers applying that fine-line of pressure on the trigger of this SIG P226.

An operator poses, dressed for what the Group calls a "Level Three Intervention." Note heavy Kevlar assault vest, Kevlar helmet, and protective goggles.

OPERATIONS

According to the Ottawa-Carleton Regional Police Service/Tactical Group mission statement, the unit is summoned to jobs within the Ottawa and Carleton area confines that do not fall within the jurisdiction of either the Royal Canadian Mounted Police (federal crimes), or JTF-2 (involving a specific federal government order), such as high-risk warrants, barricaded EDPs, and hostage situations. One team is always on patrol, while another is usually training; a third team is always on two-hour call-out status in reserve. According to the Ottawa-Carleton Regional Police Service guidelines for the Tactical Group's deployment, there are three situations to which the unit will be summoned into action:

(1) An incident where the criminals are known to be violent and could pose a "potential" threat to patrol officers (in such a scenario, the Tactical Group officers are assigned tactical command, and can use specialized non-lethal means in order to subdue, restrain and arrest the subject)

(2) The criminals are "armed and dangerous," and where the risk that firearms will be used against police officers is considered credible. (In such scenarios, the responding team deploys on "full tactical," though it is standard operating procedure that all efforts be applied in order to resolve any ordeal through peaceful means)

(3) The criminals are armed, dangerous and have either already used their weapons or have promised to do so should the police intervene. (In this, the most volatile scenario handled by the Tactical Group, a perimeter is established, a large area is evacuated, ambulances are summoned and hospital emergency rooms alerted. In such a scenario, team snipers are always deployed, and two eight-man teams activated)

A Tactical Group sniper poses with his M-16A2 5.56mm assault rifle. Used for medium-range targets (under 300 meters), the M-16 has proven itself to be a multi-faceted weapon of uncanny ease and accuracy.

A Tactical Group officer displays his Body Bunker ballistic shield—essential for entries into a room where the perp is armed, or entry into a room where a shield is required.

A Tactical Group officer peers through the sights of his Glock 9mm, fitted with a flash-light attachment for low-light room entries.

Ideal for entries and blasting doors off their hinges—the Remington 12-gauge shotgun.

For jobs involving EDPs, and even those involving armed criminals, the introduction of tear gas has been found to be a most successful "weapon of last resort" to end even the most difficult situations.

Rope work not only hones the physical ability of all members of the team, but it also provides police commanders with a unique tactical option. According to legend, there isn't a structure in Ottawa that the unit cannot climb up, or rappel down from.

Lagunari
The Italian Army's Amphibious Force
Alberto Scarpitta

As a mechanized unit, the battalion uses the VCC-2 APCs, an improved version of the M 113.

Obstacle courses, some routine and others arduous, are the staple of Lagunari training.

A perfect physical condition is essential to belonging to Lagunari's elite—the Amphibious Reconnaissance Platoon—as seen here on the isle of St. Andrew on the unit's obstacle course.

Ever since ancient times, maritime power has become an intrinsic element in how nation's wage war, how military forces are deployed to regions of strategic interest, and how nations defend and support their national interests. The increasing instability of the international landscape in the "new world order," especially in some of the emerging nations, as well as those split up along racial and religious lines, heightens the importance of a mobile and flexible military instrument which can quickly, often amphibiously, reach troubled shores and deploy decisively. Such rapid-response capabilities have, in the last few years, become increasingly important in southeastern Europe, the Mediterranean and the Middle East, where turmoil and civil war have engulfed many a nation.

Following the Second World War Italy maintained two amphibious units: the navy's San Marco Battalion, and the Lagunari Regiment, which was integral part of the army. Whereas the San Marco Battalion carried out the typical amphibious tasks related to a marine unit, operating in close-connection, in fact, with the U.S. Marine Corps and the U.S. Navy's Sixth Fleet, the Lagunari Regiment was tasked with defending the northeast maritime flank of Italy in case of invasion, or to serve as a light infantry formation in overseas deployments. The need to have a more efficient amphibious instrument, one that could meet all of Italy's regional commitments and defensive requirements, led to the creation of a joint Army-Navy Brigade, consisting of *Raggruppamento San Marco* (now a regimental task-force) and the *Reggimento Lagunari Serenissima*.

THE LAGUNARI
The Lagunari Regiment consists of a Headquarters and Headquarters Company, Recruit Training Company, a Nautical Crafts Company and the 1° Lagunari Battalion, composed of three Amphibious (rifle) and one Heavy Mortar Companies. The regiment boasts a deep-rooted dedication to professionalism and high-standards that date back to the sixteenth century—in fact, the unit is headquartered in the Lido of Venice, in the Guglielmo Pepe Barracks, an ancient building once used to house the troops of the Republic of Venice. The unit's expressed military professionalism continues to this day—only career servicemen, soldiers

With their weapons at the ready, operators from the Amphibious Recce Platoon cross a swift-moving river.

A Lagunari rifleman endures the swift currents and frigid waters during a fording exercise.

Bayonet training—Lagunari style. The emphasis on humanitarian and peace-keeping missions in recent years have only highlighted the importance of conventional combat skills when military units are sent into danger zones—even when despatched under the guise of "peace-keepers."

with experience and who have proven themselves operationally, are permitted to serve in one of the unit's rifle or mortar companies; conscripts are relegated to logistic and support tasks only. The Regimental Headquarters Company (HHC), based at Malcontenta like the 1° Battalion, comprises Headquarters, Support, Communications and Maintenance Platoons. It assures logistic, technical, sanitary and administrative support, establishes the regimental Command Post, and guarantees the communications connection between higher-ranking units and the operative companies.

THE 1° LAGUNARI BATTALION

The 1° Lagunari Battalion is commanded by a lieutenant-colonel, and consists of a small headquarters administration and four operational companies. Freed from the administrative tasks handled directly by regimental command, the unit can dedicate much of its time to hard-core combat assault training. The three amphibious companies, each commanded by a captain and each consisting of 134 men, have at their disposal sixteen VCC-2 tracked APCs (a modified version of the well-known M-113A1 that is fitted with additional steel armor protection). Each rifle company consists of Headquarters and Service Platoon (including one VCC-2 company command-post), three Rifle Platoons with four APCs each and one Anti-Tank Platoon with three tracked vehicles. The rifle platoon consists of four rifle sections for a total of thirty men, including the commander (a lieutenant or a senior NCO), the second in command and a signals officer. Each combat section consists of seven men and includes, besides the two APC crew members (a driver and a vehicle commander), the section leader and four riflemen, one of which is the squad's light machine gunner. The fourth section has only six men, lacking the vehicle commander, whose role is carried on by the

platoon sergeant. This squad is basically the anti-tank force of the platoon, operating two Milan ATGWs. The Anti-Tank Platoon of the Amphibious Rifle Company has three sections with two Milans each. In this way each rifle company has twelve Milan launchers, a weapon very effective against both armored targets or fortified positions, and crucial in offensive operations against an entrenched enemy.

THE NAUTICAL CRAFTS COMPANY

The Nautical Crafts Company is based in the isle of St. Andrew, in Venice's lagoon, and it provides the regiment with its specific marine component. In addition to the Headquarters and Service Platoon, the company includes Nautical Crafts, LVTP-7, Maintenance and Repair, Amphibious Reconnaissance and Base Support Platoons. Nautical Crafts Platoon equipment is either logistic, intended to assure isle-mainland connection, or operative. One of the unit's principal crafts is fiberglass Rigid Raiders, of which the unit possesses sixteen. With a 115-HP outboard motor they can carry eight fully-equipped men plus the coxswain, at speeds of thirty knots. The unit has just received two new LCVP landing crafts which are propelled by powerful water-jets (top spccd thirty-one knots with its complement of thirty-six fully-equipped *Lagunari*). With a crew of four, these LCVPs are supplied with a complete Kevlar ballistic armor, capable of stopping a 7.62mm NATO round at 100 meters. Six additional LCVPs are currently on order. In additions to boats and LCVPs, the amphibious mobility of the regiment is guaranteed by fifteen amphibious tracked vehicles of the LVTP-7 platoon. The replacement of these aging vehicles is currently under consideration, with the unit thinking of acquiring either smaller amphibious APCs which could carry an infantry section, or the purchasing of the AAV-7, the improved model of the LVTP-7.

The Amphibious Reconnaissance Platoon is a specialized unit trained to operate in small teams to support the main force on all amphibious deployments. Their missions include beach reconnaissance, short and medium range tactical reconnaissance, intelligence-gathering

During tactical assault entry training, members of the Lagunari 3rd Company storm a building. As is evident from the photograph, team-work, and reliance on one's fellow soldiers, is an integral element of the Lagunari's strengths.

behind enemy lines, naval and helicopter landing control, raids, shock assaults, and sabotage strikes deep behind enemy lines.

The Amphibious Reconnaissance Platoon is a purely volunteer force, and candidates hopefuls in the regiment or elsewhere in the army, must pass an eight-weeks selection course, during which both physical and

Lagunari soldiers hone their skills in the treacherous art of built-up area combat.

During training meant to prepare the force for possible deployment to the Balkans, an "enemy soldier" is stopped and searched, while a second rifleman provides cover.

A team of riflemen in defensive deployment, giving each other the highest reciprocal protection.

psychological strengths are measured and judged. Physical tests for acceptance into the unit include high-paced forced marches in full battle-kit, closely examined combat and recce patrol techniques, weapons proficiency, demolitions, swimming, the use of small boats, mountaineering and survival basic elements, deployments from helicopters and communications skills. Being selected into the unit is indeed an honor (the attrition rate is high), though acceptance only guarantees more work, for it is in the platoon that the real training begins!

The Amphibious Reconnaissance Platoon unit consists of four six-man recce teams and a squad of eight combat-divers, all NCOs, who have passed the rigorous Italian Navy dive course at Varignano, near La Spezia, home base of the famous COMSUBIN (*Commando Raggruppamento Subacqui ed Incurisori*). They use closed-circuit breathing apparatus, designed for clandestine operations in shallow waters, and other underwater delivery means.

MISSIONS

The army's amphibious troops possess a unique dual-punch capability, as they can deploy for both mechanized and amphibious operations. For many years, typical Lagunari's missions have had a tactical and defensive in nature, connected with the traditional selected mission—the defense of the north Adriatic lagoons. In such a context, combat simulations have focused on coastal defense, beach assaults, raids and small-unit infiltration. The ever changing international political and security situation, especially in the Mediterranean, the Balkans and the Middle East, has recently led to the creation of an Italian Joint Army-Navy Amphibious Brigade.

In this new operational setting the Lagunari will face very different operative challenges which will lead them to extend their acquired knowledge baggage to a wide range of new tasks. The training strategy will focus on a 360° spectrum of combat assignments—from conventional combat operations to peace-keeping, law-enforcement, emergency evacuations, humanitarian aid, and even combat support to Italian counter-terrorist and hostage-rescue operations.

The very fact that the joint force is naval trained and experienced in deploying from naval platforms, provides the Italian military in how they are actually deployed. The firepower that they can bring to bear is usually

A platoon commander receives orders from his company's executive officer during training in northern Italy.

Lagunari are always ahead of other infantrymen. Therefore they must make good use of surroundings and ground to seek cover when under enemy fire. Here, a soldier peers through the sights of his Beretta SC-70/90 5.56mm assault rifle.

Face camouflaged and body aching from a difficult forced march, a Lagunari races into firing position.

The efficiency of the Serenissima Regiment depends on the motivation and the "esprit de corps" of each Lagunari soldier, and his ability to overcome hardship—both physical and mental.

The unit's staple assault weapon, the Beretta SC-70/90 5.56mm assault rifle. Note the details of the flak jacket and the San Marco's lion badge on the uniform left sleeve.

superior to those of similar-size airborne units. Plus, and perhaps most importantly, the naval platforms provide not only firepower but a large-size mobile base of operations from where units can stand down for an extended period of time, and then, should the need arise, deploy in an instant. This of particular importance in the force's new-found role in Non-Combatant Evacuation missions (NEO), where rescue missions are not always executed with the cooperation and the consent of the host country. Often, as the case has been, such rescues are carried out in the face of clear armed opposition by the government forces or, more often, by rebel elements.

Lagunari units are now engaged in a far-reaching schedule of national, allied and multinational exercises in the Mediterranean and beyond: in Greece, Turkey, Spain, France and recently Egypt, in the Bright Star exercises with the United States military, Lagunari elements provided an amphibious special operations punch. Some elements of the regiment were deployed to Bosnia, as part of the Italian contribution to the Stabilization Force (SFOR), the NATO contingent which, by UN warrant, aims at reinforcing peace and normalizing the situation of the country. A recent Italian-Spanish agreement has reinforced the unit's regional responsibilities with increased joint training between Italian amphibious forces and their Spanish counter-parts, the *Tercio de Armada*. Perhaps, in the near future, Lagunari elements will be training with other similar forces throughout the region.

THE MEN AND THEIR TRAINING

Until recently, the Serenissima Lagunari Regiment was made up of conscripts recruited in the standing areas of the unit and selected according to strict physical and psychological requirements. The entry of the regiment into the Italian Army Deployment Forces have deeply changed its regional recruitment practices to one where soldiers from throughout the country are sought for service in the unit. In the near

Awaiting the new Minimi, the section support light machine gun is still the 7.62mm MG-42/59.

Lethal, light and Lagunari—The Milan ATGW.

future, the operational component will be made up *exclusively* of short-term volunteers (VFB), on three-year tours of duty; regulars (VSP), coming from the VFB and kept in service. Regimental recruitment teams set up shop at conscript centers in search of the right material who could adopt and excel with service in such an elite unit. Volunteers join the regiment after three months of basic training in a Volunteer Training Regiment and two more months of specialization training at the army Infantry School. New Lagunari-hopefuls attend an Amphibious Qualification Course lasting two months, in the isle of St. Andrew, run by a training cadre of the amphibious recce platoon. A similar course is given at Brindisi, with the San Marco Brigade of the Italian Navy. Instruction with the San Marco Brigade emphasizes agility and stamina, the negotiating of combat obstacle courses, and forced marches over grueling distances. Training concludes with intensive instruction in combat tactics, as well as standard operative procedures in amphibious operations. Light infantry skills are also stressed, such as highly mobile deployments, fighting in built-up areas, and deploying in small teams in hostile environments.

As a result of international missions to Lebanon, Somalia and Bosnia, peace-peaking assignment which the Italian military had played a prominent role, Fighting In Built-Up Areas (FIBUA) training has become an all-important facet in the Lagunari's training regimen. At first Lagunari learn how to overcome the most frequent obstacles correctly: for example how to assault a building covering up each other without exposing themselves to enemy fire. In FIBUA training, two-man Lagunari teams systematically and swiftly "clean out" the rooms of the targeted building: in a well-choreographed move of cover, concealment, and advancement, one soldier covers his companion's movements till the launching of the hand grenade, immediately followed by the burst of the automatic weapon and assault. These roles are then reversed until the soldiers are sufficiently proficient in this deadly game of peaking around

Passive night vision devices permit battlefield observation even in starlight conditions.

The VCC-2 is the regiment's primary APC. Fitted with additional steel armor, it has a cupola-mounted 12.7mm Browning heavy machine gun.

The VCC-2 has two firing ports on each side, permitting observation and protected firing from the relatively safe protection of ballistic shielding.

A small sniper force is attached to the regimental headquarters. They operate in the traditional sniper/observer two-man tandems. Although antiquated by some circles, the unit's precision weapon is the accurized version of the Garand M-1.

corners and eliminating any and all threats is mastered. The actions of the two-man teams are coordinated and directed by the section commander, while the light machine-gun of the unit assures the necessary fire support.

Helicopters are an irreplaceable instrument which allows the regiment to accomplish rapid concentrations of forces wherever and whenever needed. Therefore cooperation with the army aviation (AVES) is very close. Sections commanders have the responsibility for directing helicopter landings by considering sun position, wind direction and arraying their men in defense of the landing zone, in the dangerous moment of landing.

Among the Lagunari's special operations assignments requiring dedicated training is behind-enemy-lines-raids where several heavily armed mobile patrols will infiltrate enemy positions and perform commando strikes against sensitive rear-area targets, such as HQ installations, ammunition dumps and fuel supply centers. Usually, according to Lagunari procedure, such patrols consist of a dozen soldiers, equipped only with light weapons, though they may carry AT weapons and explosives, as well. Such combat operations are particularly suited to the Lagunari, because of their aggressiveness, initiative, professionalism and mission-oriented training.

WEAPONS AND EQUIPMENT

The Lagunari's weapons are the typical of those issued to Italian infantry units:

- The pistol officers and non commissioned officers are equipped with the new Beretta 92FS caliber 9mm Parabellum.
- The assault rifle is the 5.56mm Beretta SC-70/90 with folding stock. It is a very precise, modern and reliable weapon, fed by 30 rounds magazines.
- The old 7.62mm Beretta FAL BM-59 is still available in armories, and is brought along on some missions where "higher stopping power" is required.
- The section machine gun is still the well-known 7.62mm MG-42/59. It can be used either with a bi-pod, as a light support weapon, or with a tripod, for sustained fire, thanks to the rapid barrel-changes system. It is a good machine gun but requires the carrying of two separate sizes of ammunition at section level. Soon, however, the MG-42/59 will be replaced in the light support role by the Belgian Minimi that uses a two-hundred-round plastic box magazine for link-belted 5.56mm ammunition.
- At present the small regiment's sniper group makes use of the special sniper version of the venerable Garand M-1, but shortly it would be replaced by a new rifle firing the .338 Lapua Magnum cartridge, an interesting tactical compromise between the traditional 7.62mm and the heavy 12.7mm.
- The anti-tank capabilities will be improved by the new Panzerfaust-3, effective against either armored targets, bunkers or defensive fortifications, with a maximum effective range of 3-400 meters. For longer distances (up to 2,000 meters) the Milan missiles are used. Each rifle company has twelve Milans while one launcher in two will have a

The Heavy Mortar Company has eight M106 tracked vehicles for moving its own 120mm mortars.

The traditional inflatable boats are a mainstay of amphibious recon. Here it delivers a force of combat swimmers toward a target.

Co-operation between Lagunari and AVES, the army aviation, is very close. Here, an AB-205 drops a recce team into the water during assault exercises.

An assault wave is landing from the LVTP-7s amphibious tracked vehicle.

A pair of combat divers near the shore during a demolition assault training course. Divers attend a course lasting three months at the Italian Navy Dive School.

Combat swimmers, in full neoprene gear, ready to carry out a sabotage training mission.

Galileo thermal-imaging sight for full night vision.
• At present each platoon has two obsolete U.S. made 60mm M2 mortars, mainly used for training purposes. They will soon be replaced by a modern "commando" light mortar made by the Army Arsenal of Piacenza. Weighting little more than seven kilograms, it will have a maximum range of more than 1,000 meters.
• The Military Small Arms Factory in Terni is producing a 40mm grenade launcher to be fitted under one rifle in each section. It weights less than two kilos and has a range of about 400 meters.
• The Heavy Mortar Company uses eight 120mm Thomson-Brandt Model 63 weapons, with a maximum range of 6,500 meters with rocket-assisted bombs.
• The old but reliable Browning M2 12.7mm heavy machine gun may be found on top of the VCC-2 APCs but it can be used also on the ground over a tripod.
• The smallest radios used by the Lagunari in the VHF band are the RV-2/400 for section-platoon link, and the backpack-sized RV-3 for communications between platoon and company and between company and battalion or regiment.
• For longer distances HF and HF/SSB radios are used, like the SRT-178P, with data entry terminals for secure "burst" transmissions.
• Night vision devices are taking on more and more importance. The Lagunari use passive image intensifier apparatuses like night vision goggles, for personal use, weapon sights, on rifles and machine guns, and night vision binoculars, for observation duties.
• Another aid, on modern battlefield, is given by miniature GPS receivers, which can give the exact global position receiving data from a bank of satellites.

In terms of personal kit and uniform, Lagunari's battle dress is the standard army one, very similar to the American woodland design.
• Individual equipment includes a Kevlar "Fritz" helmet assuring a V50 in excess of 500 m/sec, that is the speed a certain standard splinter must have in order to obtain a fifty percent probability to pierce the protection

This rigid-hull inflatable assigned to the Nautical Crafts Platoon is used for search and rescue missions in the high Adriatic coasts.

One of the new LCVP recently acquired for use by the regiment. The Kevlar panels fixed on the upper part of the hull and on the ramp are for additional ballistic protection.

A member of the regiment wearing black beret and regimental cravat.

completely.
• Body armor a light Spain-made flak jacket is available. Made of many Kevlar HT layers, it is covered with an outer protection having the same camouflage as the BDU.
• Web gear includes a nylon belt with plastic buckle, with suspenders and shoulder straps very similar to the U.S. Alice models. As a rule, Lagunari carry two small ammunition cases for two thirty-rounds magazines, secured by a Velcro fasteners, and two larger pouches for different kinds of equipment. However, it is a very common practice to improve individual combat equipment by a private purchase of pouches and combat field packs of different origins.
• In case of engagement in hot and arid climates, a four-color uniform with a khaki ground and green, brown and light brown spots is available. In these situations flak jackets and helmet covers with the same camouflage are also distributed. Web gears are sable-colored.
• When the joint Army-Navy Amphibious Brigade is operative, it is probable that the Lagunari will receive San Marco Regiment's battle dress uniforms, considered to be of higher quality than the standard Army ones. Light, comfortable and processed to limit infrared radiation emitted by the human body, these uniforms can be particularly used in hot climates, like in the Mediterranean basin, thanks to their "hot" and quite light five-color camouflage.

Like every elite force, the Army amphibious troops are very proud of their traditions and the symbols representing them.
• The San Marco's winged lion is the distinguishing mark of the regiment. It is an ancient military symbol of the Republic of Venice. Yellow, on a plastic red background, it is worn on the BDU uniform, on the left shoulder (a green and black fabric subdued version is now available). The same insignia, affectionately called "Mao", in enameled metal, is worn on the left breast pocket of the summer shirt.
• The winged lion symbol is also on the regimental cravat, in the traditional red and gold colors.
• Lagunari's beret is black, bearing a metal badge reproducing an anchor on two crossed rifles. It is a clear reference to their belonging to infantry, of which the Lagunari are the newest specialty, and to their special amphibious skills.

The Klepper, a traditional tool of naval special warfare units, is among the Lagunari's most effective infiltration tools.

Present Lagunari arise from "fanti da mar" which were, since 1550, the Venetian troops employed on Serenissima ships as landing and assaulting contingents. The force, a regiment made up of ten companies, consisted of 5,000 men which distinguished themselves in many war actions. Modern Lagunari as part of Italian infantry were born after the second world war as a force designed to operate in the shallow coastal waters around Venice and the other river estuaries. For these tasks a mixed Army-Navy force was created in 1951 in the Lido of Venice. In 1957 the Navy component left the unit, which became an Army Task Force composed of three amphibious battalions. On May 24, 1964 the Task Force, conveniently reinforced, became the 1° Reggimento Lagunari Serenissima, with three amphibious battalions (Marghera, Piave and Isonzo), one tank battalion and amphibious vehicles and small boats units. In 1975 a deep reorganization of the Italian Army caused the disbanding of the regiment and the rise of a new Amphibious Troops Command on two battalions, the Serenissima and the Sile. In 1992 a new reorganization gave rise to the rebirth of the regiment, now on a single battalion.

1st LAGUNARI REGIMENT

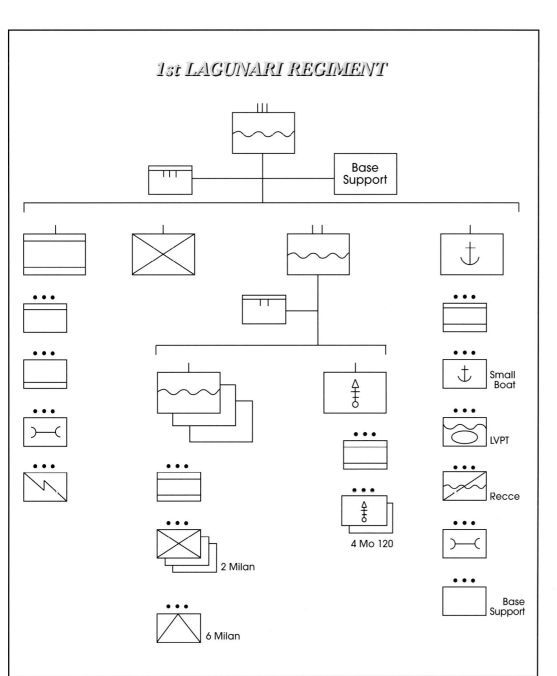

The elite Amphibious Recce Platoon patch, worn on the right shoulder.

Lagunari's patch in subdued version.

Base Support

Small Boat

LVPT

Recce

Base Support

4 Mo 120

2 Milan

6 Milan

Lagunari's patch, worn on the left shoulder of the BDU.

Lagunari's San Marco winged lion, in enamelled metal, worn on the left brest pocket of the summer shirt.

Lagunari's beret badge.

Argentina's Cops of Last Resort:
"The State Police Seccion Fuerzas Especiales"

Gilles Rivet

A strike team from the Seccion Fuerzas Especiales deploys during dynamic entry training. Note Heckler and Koch 40mm MZP-1 multi-purpose pistol used by the entry team.

"If you want peace, prepare for war!"

Ezeiza, the suburbs of Buenos Aires, 08:00 Hours: The February morning brought with the sun's first light the true meaning of the South American summer—heat, humidity, and the glaring reality that the thermometer would breach the 35º (C) mark before 10:00 A.M. Yet just before sunrise, something even more explosive than the heat was permeating through the humid air. It was the sound of Heckler and Koch MP5s being fired, SIG P226 9mm handguns launching three-round bursts of fire, and the cadence of orders, issued in a rhythmic Spanish, demanding that the assembled group of men dressed in black do their tasks faster, better, and with greater concentration. Welcome to the world of Argentina's super cops, and the State Police special operations force of last resort.

In Argentina, a land known for the vastness of its frontiers, the beauty of its women, and the potential turmoil of its politics, two distinctive and quite different police special operations units are employed to guarantee that violent situations with the potential for tragedy are handled efficiently and effectively. First and foremost, there is the *Brigada Halcon* of the Policia Bonaerense, a semi-national hostage-rescue and counter-terrorist team activated by the Ministry of Interior and called upon to respond to any and all hostage incidents (especially those on board buses, trains, planes and boats), sensitive location security, VIP and Dignitary Protection, and deployment overseas to safeguard Argentine interests threatened by terrorist attack (such as embassies, consulates and visiting political figures). The primary area of operation for *Brigada Halcon* is an urban setting—the cities and towns around the Argentine capital. The second unit, the *Seccion Fuerzas Especiales*, is a para-military force under the jurisdiction and command

of the Ministry of Defense's State Police—the National Gendarmerie, similar in mission, scope, abilities and resources to the Italian Carabinieri and the French Gendarmerie Nationale. The Argentina State Police's area of responsibility is the countryside, the rolling green hills, and the thick and dense forest and valleys of the inner heartland.

In most countries, there are often two or even three national hostage-rescue teams that compete for large-scale operations; usually, the competition exists between a national military unit, and a police or Gendarmerie force. In Israel, for example, there is great competition between *Sayeret Mat'kal,* the General Staff Reconnaissance Unit of the Israel Defense Forces and the Special Police Unit (the *Ya'ma'm*) of the National Police. In Italy, *great* competition exists between the Carabinieri's GIS and the National Police NOCS, while in France similar professional and operational rivalries exist between the Gendarmerie's GIGN, and the National Police RAID team. And, in Spain, there is great operational competition between the GEO, and the UEI—two units many counter-terrorist experts consider among the world's premier teams. In Argentina, like in most other countries, the decision as to which team is called is almost exclusively a political one—determined by personal and logistical considerations. Yet in Argentina, the national government possesses, within its national counter-terrorist order of battle, two of perhaps the finest intervention squads in the world. Argentina possesses a luxury that is the envy of many a nation.

Because its primary area of responsibility is the countryside, the *Seccion Fuerzas Especiales* has enjoyed a variety of work few national police forces encounter, and a myriad of challenges and threats few counter-terrorist teams ever get to face for real. Created in 1986, the

With their arsenal of Heckler and Koch MP5 variants at the ready, a Seccion Fuerzas Especiales *entry team prepares to enter the great unknown of a room that has yet to be cleared.*

During aircraft take-down exercises near Buenos Aires, a two-man Seccion Fuerzas Especiales *tandem covers another team of operators about to enter the aircraft with their Heckler and Koch MP5 SD3.*

A two-man Seccion Fuerzas Especiales *sniper team peers through the Schmidt & Bender scopes of their SIG-Sauer SSG-2000 rifle.*

Seccion Fuerzas Especiales has encountered Hizballah terrorists operating near the Bolivian and Paraguayan borders, to drug smugglers using the mountains and jungles as ideal caches for their prized stashes, and protective armies. The back roads and small rural villages of Argentina can be as picturesque as a journeyman's postcards, and as treacherous and unforgiving as the wild west.

As a result of the dangers and diverse geographic areas of responsibility within the Ministry of Defense police jurisdiction, the *Seccion Fuerzas Especiales* is a multi-faceted and multi-talented force of operators trained in everything from high-speed take-downs and arrests on mountain dirt roads, to explosive room entries. Firearms proficiency isn't just a professional requirement with the *Seccion Fuerzas Especiales*, it's a unit passion. Every morning, before the work day commences, unit operators rush to the range to perfect their nearly flawless marksmanship scores. The operators shoot the weapons in the unit arsenal, from the SIG Sauer P226 to the Heckler and Koch MP5, with limited ammunition allowances on virtually a daily cycle. Even the snipers, armed with the lethal SSG 2000 .308 rifle, do not miss a morning's workout on the trigger. Other elements of the profession that are routinely practiced by the unit include: (1) hostage-rescue and tubular assaults, (2) jungle and forest operations, (3) high-speed and evasive driving maneuvers, (4) heliborne insertion and operations, (5) long-range reconnaissance, (6) riverine and amphibious operations, and, (7) EOD instruction. Recently, the unit has extended great effort to hone its skills in the art of aircraft take-downs. Even though the *Brigada Halcon* is trained to execute the

Stoic portrait of a Seccion Fuerzas Especiales *operator about to deploy a 40mm tear-gas round from his MZP-1.*

assault and rescue of any aircraft hijacked in Argentina, the *Seccion Fuerzas Especiales* is also on-call to respond to any aircraft diversion. Much of the unit's interest in aircraft assault stems from the incident in Marseilles, in December 1994, when operators from France's GIGN assaulted an A300 Airbus hijacked to the city by Algerian terrorists and rescued over 150 hostages in a brilliant display of tactical talent and national determination. Not only did the *Seccion Fuerzas Especiales* use the incident in Marseilles as a call to arms, but it began an intensive training-regimen meant to ready the force to any potential hijacking incident inside Argentina. The unit, working closely with the national air carriers, soon began appearing at major airports in the early A.M. hours to learn the art of aircraft take-downs. Breaching the obstacles to hijacked aircraft as diverse as the Boeing 747 and Fokker 27 were taught, mastered and perfected. The unit also ventured to France to train alongside the GIGN. The unit, interestingly enough, has also trained alongside elements from the American counter-terrorism community, as well as other South American intervention teams. It should also be mentioned the *Seccion Fuerzas Especiales* enjoys a unique and close-knit working relationship with the Spanish national team, the GEO, and has trained with them on a regular basis.

After a grueling morning of aircraft take-downs, a team of Seccion Fuerzas Especiales *operators display both national and unit pride.*

Being a member of the *Seccion Fuerzas Especiales* is, undoubtedly, one of the most difficult goals any policeman can set for himself. To be one of the elite, one of the unit's forty-four operators, a State Police officer must be a sergeant, and have at least five years of exemplary service. All volunteers must be in "ideal" physical condition, and must be able to pass a grueling physical fitness examination that includes, a swimming test, a foot-race, combat-shooting, and an obstacle course. Training, for the few who make it past these barriers, as well as the psychological tests and the extensive (and discriminating) oral reviews, is

six months long divided into two three month curriculum terms. Beyond the "routine" elements of the profession taught to *Seccion Fuerzas Especiales* candidates, operator-hopefuls are also taught rope-skills, camouflage, long-range pursuits skills for jungle-operations, parachuting, explosive entries and the use of pyrotechnics, and cold-killing. Following the end of the instructional period, all those who have survived the training (and about eighty-percent do not!) undergo an eight-month probationary period where they are assigned to an instructor (usually a senior member of the unit) and await their turn to join the regular force.

The few heart-pounding seconds between silence and explosive entry—a Seccion Fuerzas Especiales *team awaits the order of enter!*

In SWAT work, the most feared words are always "Do it again!" Here, after nearly a dozen hours of aircraft take-down training, a Seccion Fuerzas Especiales *element does it "once again!"*

Close-up photograph of an operator deploying his MZP-1 40mm grenade launcher.

The business-end of being at the wrong end of an aircraft hijacking. The ballistic body bunker is useful for that first explosive second of entry, but a burden inside the cramped and confined spaces of an aircraft aisle.

The forty-four men team is divided into two operational sections, with each consisting of two groups who, each possess two operational assault teams. According to *Seccion Fuerzas Especiales* and State Police standard operating procedure, during "call-outs," twenty-two men respond; included in this force are two snipers, and additional special equipment personnel, armed with a variety of unique assault gears (including crossbows, and mortars). The unit's EOD detachment, known by the acronym of GEDEX, is also deployed to all call-out incidents requiring the presence of a *Seccion Fuerzas Especiales* operational section. Transport in the unit is divided among a fleet of 4x4 all-terrain vehicles, as well as C-130s and Huey choppers of the Argentinean Air Force that are on-call, twenty-four hours a day, to respond to any incident inside Argentina. Also, it should be noted, *Seccion Fuerzas Especiales* are required to live less than two kilometers from the unit's home base of

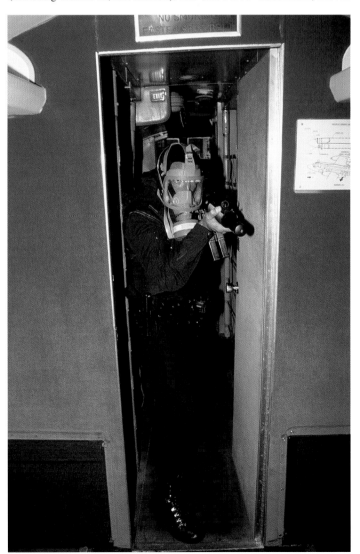

A hijacker's worst-nightmare—looking down the silenced barrel of an MP5 a split-second before 9mm termination.

A Seccion Fuerzas Especiales *operator poses for the camera during unit jungle training. Note U.S. parachutist wings.*

Ezeiza, and are constantly connected to the State Police command by cellular phones and pagers. There is always a team, on an immediate deployment basis, standing at the ready to be the first responders to any national emergency.

Commanders in the State Police, realizing the success and unique operational abilities that the *Seccion Fuerzas Especiales* have provided to the nation since their creation in 1986, are determined to expand the unit to a force of over sixty operators in the coming months; and, there has also been talk about potentially raising the number of officers in the unit to 100 by the turn of the century. The bombings of the Israeli embassy and Jewish cultural center in Buenos Aires have proven that Argentina, a nation at the southern tip of the Americas, is not immune to the threats of international terrorism originating from the Middle East and even points beyond. And, with a history of autocratic rule and violent internal opposition, Argentina is also a nation well aware of the threats from internal terrorist elements, as well. Perhaps at no time in Argentina's history have the services of its super cops been so urgently needed.

Indistinguishable from the remaining foliage and landscape, Seccion Fuerzas Especiales *train year-round in jungle combat operations and the art of camouflage.*

The fashion of counter-terrorism— Seccion Fuerzas Especiales *operators dressed in a variety of black Nomex and leather gear, pose for the camera outside the unit's HQ in Ezeiza.*

His SIG-Sauer P226 at the ready, a Seccion Fuerzas Especiales *bunker-man prepares to make dynamic entry.*

Heliborne insertion is a must for jungle-terrain special operations—as this two-man tandem of Seccion Fuerzas Especiales *operators display near the Bolivian frontier.*

About to deploy tear gas, a Seccion Fuerzas Especiales entry team assumes a cover position behind the team's bunker man.

Rope work isn't considered a skill in the Seccion Fuerzas Especiales, it's considered a religion. Here, lurched atop a ledge at precarious heights, an operator trains his Heckler and Koch MP5K A5 on a targeted window.

Utilizing the "Australian Rappel," a Seccion Fuerzas Especiales operator armed with a Heckler and Koch HK53 5.56mm submachine gun proves that the shortest distance between two points is "straight down."

Following the successful completion of aircraft take-down training on light commuter aircraft, two Seccion Fuerzas Especiales operators ponder the subject of the next day's instruction—the almighty Boeing 747.

Norway's Finnmark Jaegers

Yves Debay

A three-man Jaeger team awaits a flight of an "enemy" warplane during anti-aircraft operations training in the frozen landscape of northern Norway. The Stinger operator is supported by a spotter, and a grenadier armed with a G-3/40mm grenade launcher combination.

In the great white north of Norway, where only the strongest can survive, a new unit of elite solider has been born. They are the rangers of the Finnmark Regiment's 7th Jaeger Company, and they are Norway's trip-wire in case of an invasion from the east through terrain and climatic conditions that few men, and machines, can traverse. The unit's primary mission is to delay and harass any invasion by using guerrilla-tactics and small-unit strikes against enemy strategic targets to buy the precious commodity of time so that the conventional forces of Norway's 6th Regiment can establish a first-line of defense, at predisposed position, in more favorable terrain. It is, perhaps, one of the most unique military formations in the world today—trained not to prevail or vanquish, instead the force is simply a human minefield—designed to deter and delay an enemy's advance at any costs.

Norway's 7th Jaeger Company is responsible for the Kirkenes Region in the far northern-most stretches of Norway, a desolate chunk of territory that shares a common frontier with the former Soviet Union, and that is completely covered in snow from September to May. In the spring and the summer, the temperature hovers between freezing and 45°(F). In winter, the temperature descends to an unimaginable -40°(F). The terrain has been referred to, by local military commanders, as a white desert, and indeed, its frozen, rock hard surface, is ideal for armored warfare. It is also the type of terrain well-suited for special operations forces. Beyond the need for a commando force that can meet and challenge any invader in such inhospitable conditions, the unit is meant to instill a psychological warning onto any enemy—"if we are capable of surviving in this frozen hell, living off the land frozen out of any livable means, then we are truly invincible."

The 7th Jaeger Company is an experimental unit. Drawn upon the finest soldiers, the strongest psychologically and physically, of the Finnmark Regiment, they are trained to locate an enemy's weak-spots, exploit them with speed and stealth, and to attack them with merciless fury. The 7th is particularly trained for selective strikes against strategic targets in the enemy rear—SCUD missile launchers, mobile divisional headquarters, logistic and ammunition dumps, radar stations, and forward helicopter landing positions.

In the frozen forests and tundra of northern Norway, there are two means of transportation that are fast and reliable—skis and snowmobiles. Both are used to a great extent by the Jaegers. The 7th Jaeger Company possesses sixty-eight "skidoos," or Yamaha Viking snowmobiles. The Viking weighs in at 770 lb. and can reach a top-speed of eighty kilometers an hour in the deepest of snows. Easy to drive, ideal for maneuverability in the often impassable barriers of snow drifts and sheets of rock hard, though slippery ice, the vehicle can easily carry two fully equipped soldiers along with over 450 lb. of equipment; it can also drag a trailer loaded to captivity with an additional 420 lb. of equipment. The snowmobile's fuel-frugal engine permits the soldiers to traverse long distances on single tanks of petrol, though the Jaegers strategically hide ammunition and fuel supplies throughout the frozen wilderness in hidden dumps. The Jaegers learned this supply and conceal method from the masters at long-range commando strikes—Captain David Stirling's legendary Long Range Desert Patrol, though the Norwegians never had to endure the heat and dust of the desert, and Captain Stirling was never confronted with wind-chills of -50°(F). Well hidden by trees, boulders and the camouflaging anonymity of the snow, the Jaegers are able to

A close-up photo of the Stinger team, as well as their ubiquitous Yamaha "skidoo" snowmobile—the true camel of the white desert.

Excellent photograph of the water-proof protective smocks worn by Jaeger personnel in the great white expanses of northern Norway. Note G-3 rifle with winter camouflage applied.

locate the buried supplies with pinpoint accuracy by using GPS (Global Positioning System).

Clearly in order to be a Jaeger, a soldier must be comfortable with the snow and frigid elements. Norwegians are, by the geographic-positioning of their country, slaves to the winter and cold, and they have learned to excel and to enjoy the paradise of their winter-wonderland. Yet functioning, let along surviving, as a combat unit in the sub-freezing climate is different than enjoying a mid-morning cross-country skiing trip with a group of friends. The soldiers must not only learn to function in the weather and to execute their combat assignments in the bone-snapping cold, they must learn to survive in these elements with the minimum of equipment and shelter. There are no ski lodges after a day's training in the snow, no warm fireplaces and dry rooms. The Jaegers must learn to ignore the frigid and often bone-numbing conditions when lurking in the snow hunting for an enemy troop column, or when trying to sleep in a damp tent with wind-chills that can cause frostbite in minutes.

Based at Porsanger, the Jaeger company commander takes great effort in *winterizing* the 124 men in his command to the point where the thermometer does not become an enemy on the field of battle. Men are of course perfectly trained to survive and to fight by great cold, and the

unit's three platoons (*Tropp*) of riflemen, along with the command and mortar platoon are pushed toward the human endurance envelope throughout the eight cold months of heavy-duty training. Each platoon consists of three eight-man teams equipped with fifteen snowmobiles. Each team has a specialized skill used as a cohesive ballistic punch by the unit—one crew is trained as marksman and observer, another is responsible for the Carl Gustav 84mm anti-tank rocket and ERYX ATGW. In each eight-man team, three Jaegers are equipped with G-3 7.62mm assault rifles fitted with 40mm grenade launchers, three are armed with Heckler and Koch MP-5 9mm submachine guns, two operate as snipers with the Våpensmia A/S NM-149 7.62mm sniping rifle; soon, however, Jaeger snipers will deploy 12.7mm precision weapons. There is also one Carl Gustav of 84mm, and ERYX antitank missile, an anti-aircraft Stinger missile. Snowmobile drivers are equipped with night-vision goggles (NVG) NM-117 and three laser range-finder are equally in endowment in the section. The fifteen-men of the company's mortar platoon are equipped with four Royal Ordnance L-16 81mm mortars.

The company is trained in calling in aerial strikes from the F-16s of the Royal Norwegian Air Force (RNoAF), as well as a medevac mission. The unit works closely with a fleet of specially equipped Bell-412 choppers. Most importantly, perhaps, the snowmobiles are easily air transportable.

Yamaha Viking "skidoo" in action in the frozen solitude of the Kirkenes province to more than 600 kilometers north of the Arctic circle. Mobility, speed and firepower constitute of course the main advantage of capable Norwegian Rangers to hit and then disappear immediately in the white immensity.

Interesting close-up photograph of a two-man Carl Gustav AT team, racing through a snowy path on their Viking snowmobiles.

A fuel store, usually well-concealed by the camouflaging white blanket of snow, is uncovered for a quick pit-stop while the unit breaks from an operational patrol.

Stoic photograph of a grenadier, his determined expression not revealing the sub-freezing conditions, poses for the camera—his G-3/40mm grenade launcher combination slung across his shoulder.

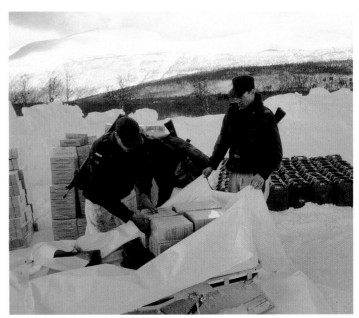

Hidden fuel depots, where supplies are pre-stored and hidden from an enemy's view, provide Jaeger teams with tremendous operational autonomy to teams in patrol. A team can remain in the field for two weeks, in temperatures of -40°(F), without resupply.

At a forward CP, a team leader radios to HQ with the findings of an operational patrol near the frontier.

Close-up view of the G-3 fitted with a grenade launcher attachment—a Norwegian special forces favorite.

All snipers and observers in the Jaeger company also carry the Heckler and Koch MP-5 9mm submachine gun.

A Jaeger sniper peers through the sights of his bolt-action NM-149.

Easily transportable by snowmobile, the RO L-16 81mm mortar provides the lightly armed Jaeger teams with lethal firepower.

During live-fire exercises, a RO L-16 81mm crew prepares to lace a target with HE ordnance.

The World's Oldest And Most Volatile Beat!
Special Operations Policing in Israel

Samuel M. Katz

Ya'ma'm *operators deploy atop a roof-top during unit maneuvers in Central Israel. (Israel National Police)*

"There isn't a corner of the city that I am scared to walk through," proclaims a cocky and confident Dubi. A Jerusalem native who has spent very few of his thirty-one-years outside the confines of the City of David, he knows every inch of the city, every crevice, every one of the city's tremendous glories. Dubi's bravado comes well-warranted, but it is a statement worthy of fool's gold in the City of Gold. Dubi happens to be a police officer walking the Jerusalem beat, but he's not just any cop, he's a super cop. While most cops carry pistols, Dubi carries an assault rifle, completed with two loaded magazines and a sniper scope. No wonder why the city seems so safe to him. Dubi happens to be a *Pakad* or Inspector in an elite patrol unit designed to deter the outbreak of violence and hostile terrorist activity in perhaps the most volatile tinder box on the planet. He works in a city which three religions call their own, a divided capital and epicenter of the Arab-Israeli struggle, and a city where tourists and residents are occasionally stabbed by terrorists. Any incident, from an arrest not handled properly to a shooting can have international implications. A Jerusalem cop needs to be sensitive and alert, part diplomat and part counter-terrorist operator.

Today, terrorism is but one of the "major" headaches encountered by the Israel National Police—*Mishteret Yisrael*. There are massive car thefts inside Israel, an explosion of organized crime courtesy of new immigrants from the former Soviet Union, a thriving drug trade courtesy of smugglers in Lebanon and Egypt, and astounding jump in rape and sexual assault cases, and an overall rise in the murder and robbery rate that has caused many senior police officials significant concern over recent months. All this as Israel prepares to expand as a major economic and political force in the Middle East and in Europe as a result of the peace accords signed with the Palestine Liberation Organization and the Kingdom of Jordan.

The "Jewish Police Force" has come a long way since Prime Minister David Ben-Gurion created the national police in March 1948. The cop on the beat used to be a fixture in Israeli life, dressed in his khaki uniform, peaked cap and silver metal badge in hand. He used to respond to neighborhood disputes and petty crimes but nothing major. Terrorism used to be restricted to the frontier areas and the Occupied Territories, and organized crime, drive-by shootings, the narcotics trade, uncontrollable robberies, massive auto-thefts only happened in the United States and Europe. Citizens used to only call the "100" emergency number when suspicious looking individuals, possibly terrorists, were seen lurking in their neighborhoods or to report a suspicious object to the bomb squad. Today, "100" is called to report kids smoking hashish and reports of violent robbers. Israeli citizens no longer purchase handguns to protect their homes against Palestinian terrorists but against Jewish burglars, as well. Israeli police men and women have retired their .38 caliber revolvers and aluminum whistles in exchange of Kevlar flak vests and Car-15 5.56mm assault rifles. Policing in the Jewish State has changed dramatically over the past fifty years and, if current trends continue, the job will grow more dangerous and challenging in the years to come.

From the inception of *Mishteret Yisrael*—the Israel Police—law enforcement was entrusted to a single national police entity. The Israel Police had responsibility for preventing and detecting crime; apprehending suspects, charging them, and bringing them to trial; keeping law and order; and enforcing traffic control. Since 1974, following the Ma'alot Massacre when an Israel Defense Force commando unit stormed a school seized by Palestinian terrorists and nearly thirty students were killed, the Israel Police has also been responsible for internal security inside Israel, including the prevention of border infiltration and hostage rescue. The Israel Police had been, from

52

A Ya'ma'm *operator negotiates a tower obstacle during physical fitness training. (Israel National Police)*

1948 to 1984 under the jurisdiction of the Ministry of the Interior, though is now controlled under a cabinet-level body known as the Ministry of Police. Since the inception of the Israel Police in 1948, the force has gone from a minuscule entity of several thousand officers and investigators to a sizable and highly-professional force numbering over 22,000 officers and detectives, including nearly 5,000 Border Guards.

The Israel Police can be separated into two distinctive entities—the "blue," or regular police, and the "green police," the Border Guards and

The Ya'ma'm *staple, the Ta'as Jericho 941. (Courtesy: Israel National Police)*

their specialized units. For the "Blue Police" the country is divided into six major commands, known as a *Machoz* or District, with each district responsible for sub-districts (known in Hebrew as *Merchav*); only the Jerusalem District, is an entity onto itself. The busiest of the districts is Tel Aviv. Israel's largest city and suburban sprawl is the population center of the nation and also Israel's most criminally active. The Northern District, with three sub-districts, includes the large port city of Haifa, the Galilee region, and the Amaqim zone. The Southern District, with three sub-districts, controls a region including the southern coast cities of Ashdod and Ashqelon, Be'ersheba in the Negev Desert, and the volatile agricultural collectives and cooperatives around the Gaza Strip and the Palestinian autonomy zone (the Shimshon sub-district). The Shai District is responsible for policing the Occupied Territories (both Jewish settlements and Arab towns and cities) and is divided into the Judea sub-district and the Samaria sub-district. Law-enforcement in the West Bank and Gaza Strip was never an easy task and compounded by the Palestinian terrorist campaign and the Israeli military and security service response. Nevertheless, from 1967 until the Israeli withdrawal from Gaza in 1994, Egyptian criminal law applied to the resident of the Gaza Strip, Jordanian criminal law applied to residents of the West Bank and Israeli law applied to Israeli citizens in both Gaza and the West Bank.

The sub-districts exercise authority over individual police stations, though most operations, including the investigation of crimes, are carried out at the police station level (what would be comparable to the police precinct in American terms), subject to guidance form the appropriate

Ya'ma'm *officers engage one another in a very-real bone-bruising exercise in Krav-Maga. (Israel National Police)*

The Ya'ma'm's *live-fire range. (Israel National Police)*

functional bureau of the national headquarters in Jerusalem. The principal bureaus of the national headquarters set-up are Operations Divisions responsible for patrol, traffic, internal security and bomb-disposal work; Investigations, tasked with criminal investigation, intelligence, criminal identification, fraud, and organized crime; Administration, in charge of personnel, training, communications, and finance. Each division has subordinate offices at the district levels and answer directly to the *Mateh Ha'Artzi*—National Headquarters in Jerusalem.

Recruitment and training criteria for the Israel Police are quite similar to those for national conscription—indeed, all recruits to the police are individuals who have successfully completed their years of mandatory national service. Traditionally, because of low police wages in relation to other employment opportunities the force traditionally encountered difficulties in filling its ranks. It is possible to enter the police force at any one of four levels—senior officer, officer, non-commissioned officer, or constable—depending on education and experience. Except for certain specialized professionals, such as lawyers and accountants who deal with white collar offenses, most police entering as officers had relevant military experience and had held equivalent military ranks. Advancement is based principally on success in training courses, and to a lesser degree on seniority and the recommendation of the immediate superior officer. Assignment to the officers' training course was preceded by a rigorous selection board interview. The National Police School is located in Galilee, at Shefaraam, southwest of Nazareth, and the basic officer's course lasts six-month and covers the laws of the country, investigation, traffic control, and other aspects of police work—

both tactical and preventative. Sergeants school lasts six months, and officers course, including seminar-type work and on-the-job experience in investigation, traffic, patrolling, and administration, lasts ten months. Years ago, when crime-fighting was a simpler matter, the Israel Police placed less emphasis on physical fitness, self-defense, and marksmanship than police organizations in other countries, but that philosophy is changing as the Israel Police finds itself encountering an increasingly violent criminal element—from Hamas terrorists seeking martyrdom to Russian mobsters from the *Organizatsiya* that have set-up base in Israel controlling gambling, prostitution and narcotics enterprises in the large cities. Recently, the Israel Police has begun recruiting soldiers just out of their three-years of national service who served in reconnaissance or elite combat units. Today, tremendous emphasis is placed on a policeman's—and policewoman's—physical ability and even cops on the beat are looking like SWAT officers; a stringent physical fitness course is a prerequisite requirement for getting through the academy. Many police stations now boast gyms and weight-training rooms, and the police Physical Fitness School has its own advanced combat course firing range where physical aptitude and tactical shooting skills can be nurtured and combined.

Two Ya'sa'm officers, CAR-15s in hand, armed with tear-gas launchers and Uzi 9mm submachine guns, prepare to enter a suspected terrorist location in East Jerusalem.

A Ya'sa'm team commander stands watch over a row of windows, as he clutches his CAR-15 5.56mm assault rifle, modified to fire rubber bullets.

Police patrols in Israel are not merely responsive but rather deterrent in nature, as well. The sight of the blue cap and flak vest bearing the word "Mishtera" (Police) presents a symbol of law and order and an immediate tactical response.

54

As Ya'sa'm *officers are often encountered with heavily-armed individuals, as well as those wielding explosives or Molotov cocktails, many officers carry scopes on their CAR-15 5.56mm assault rifles.*

Watching as a steady stream of motorists whiz by at high speeds, a Ya'sa'm *officer keeps an eye out for a suspicious vehicle wanted by the police in regard to a terrorist incident.*

In producing a modern police force that is capable to tactically respond to criminal matters, the Israel Police has formed several elite and specialized units. In the first years of the Palestinian uprising, the *Ya'ma'm*, the Border Guard/Israel Police hostage-rescue unit found itself functioning virtually exclusively in Arab East Jerusalem, primarily in the Old City of Jerusalem in the confines of the el-Aqsa mosque. Demonstrations by fundamentalists, often where weapon were deployed, characterized the Jerusalem front of the uprising. The *Ya'ma'm*, trained in lightning fast assaults, now found itself containing massive demonstrations and riots—often through non-lethal means. In one instance, a *Ya'ma'm* operator was kidnapped by a mob of worshippers and brought inside the mosque where he was savagely beaten and robbed of his weapon and radio. A stand-off ensued and with the media watching, *Ya'ma'm* officers were able to convince the cleric of mosque that it was in the best interest of the faithful to return the officer and his weapon immediately. The "Battle for Jerusalem," as many police officer called it, was difficult and tense, and resulted in the formation of a special police unit to deal with volatile riot and mob situations. That unit was the *Ya'sa'm* (Hebrew acronym for Special Patrol Unit)—units attached to district and sub-district commands that initiated tactical patrols through volatile areas in order to quell the seeds of disturbance, and should a demonstration be out of control (be in a hotbed neighborhood for Hamas or in an ultra-Orthodox Jewish neighborhood), be called in to end matters through non-lethal means if possible, and lethal means if required. Characteristic in their khaki fatigues and blue baseball caps, *Ya'sa'm* officers carry heavy weapons (Uzi and CAR-15) on their patrols and usually saturate an area of patrol with their presence. By American standards, the *Ya'sa'm* can be considered part anti-crime, part SWAT, and specialists in their terrain they cover. In Jerusalem, for example, unit personnel know every nook and cranny of the Old City and the Arab eastern section of the city, and the boulevards and neighborhoods of the Jewish western half. In the Tel Aviv District, *Ya'sa'm* officers work in drug infested neighborhoods and slums raiding known drug hang-outs and providing deterrence by their very visual patrols. In the Galilee, the Northern District's *Ya'sa'm* is a rural mobile response team, functioning with great skill and efficiency against drug-smuggling operations receiving their narcotics from over the Lebanese frontier.

One of the most unique elements within the *Ya'sa'm* is one of the world's truly unique counter-terrorist units—the counter-terrorist motorcycle squad. Cops in Jerusalem have always walked an impossible beat. They work in a city that is holy to three major religions, caught in the transition of time between its ancient past and a high-tech modern future, and is the capital of the State of Israel. Jerusalem has also been one of the world's most blood-soaked targets for terrorist attack. From grenades abandoned in shopping stalls inside a bustling market, to gunmen unleashing a point-blank burst of AK-47 fire into a crowd of pedestrians, to a suicide bomber turning a commuter bus into a death trap for twenty innocent civilians, police commanders in Jerusalem have had to fight a war of national survival waged on their city's streets, as well as maintain law and order with the routine elements of police work, such as anti-crime patrols and traffic enforcement. Protecting a city of 300,000, as well as the facets of government, from terrorist attack has not been an easy job and it has forced the top police brass in Israel to come up with innovative and often revolutionary means for coping with impossible scenarios. The Jerusalem Police Bomb-Squad has always been the busiest in Israel and considered among the world's best. The *Ya'sa'm*, Hebrew acronym for Special Patrol Unit, was first tested in Jerusalem as a mobile tactical force to patrol sensitive areas and to quell any significant public disturbances before they erupted into full-fledged chaos; today there are *Ya'sa'm* units attached to each district and sub-district command. The Anti-Terrorist Motorcycle Unit is just the latest innovation to be tested, perfected and deployed by the Jerusalem Police.

As they walk their beat in teams of multiple officers, several team leaders link up for an impromptu field briefing at a busy East Jerusalem interchange.

Israeli Police Commissioner Assaf Hefetz, a pioneering counter-terrorist operator and officer, and, along with Jerusalem Police Chief Commander Arieh Amit, the architect of the Jerusalem Anti-Terrorist Motorcycle Unit. (Israel National Police)

The current police commissioner is Assaf Hefetz, a veteran special operations officer and the man who founded the Israeli Police national counter-terrorist force, known as the *Ya'ma'm*. During a trip to Turkey in 1994, Commissioner Hefetz witnessed a display by a special police squad in Istanbul and Ankara that dealt with counter-terrorist duties. The unit was a small force, of only thirty officers, yet it covered territory with speed and firepower. Since most terrorists in Turkey deploy from motorcycles, speedy two-wheelers afford ninety-mile-per-hour-plus transportation for assassins armed with automatic rifles, responding police units found themselves incapable of catching up to the perpetrators with any hope of stopping them, or engaging them before their planned escape. Many of Ankara's and Istanbul's narrow streets and alleyways hampered vehicular pursuits and afforded a fleeing terrorist a maze-like hiding area. Jerusalem had many similar characteristics and Commissioner Hefetz was inspired by the notion of sending out heavily armed operators on high-speed bikes. Having sat through traffic jams in the capital more often than he'd like to, Commissioner Hefetz realized that the overcrowded thoroughfares of the capital have often hindered police response times to major incidents. Commissioner Hefetz also realized that the Old City of Jerusalem, with its narrow descending alleyways, corridors and dead ends, was not suited for police vehicles, and foot pursuits often reached the scene too late for officers to affect an arrest or engagement with arrest bombers or terrorists. The tactical motorcycle unit was a novel solution to an existing scenario that needed to be addressed. Commissioner Hefetz conferred with Commander Arieh Amit, the maverick Jerusalem Police chief, about creating such a unit in the capital. Amit, always ready for new ideas, the more innovative and exciting the better, contacted his operations chief and the *Ya'sa'm* commander. Within weeks, the unit was an operational plan with a commanding officer, a cadre of instructors, and a shopping list of bikes, weapons and gear that needed to be purchased. The new force's objective—to reduce the response time to ongoing or developing terrorist incidents, and to be able to provide a tactical deterrence, response and pursuit-ability.

The first requirement of the unit was speed. In the precarious world of police tactical response, a unit's response time is just as important a factor in resolving a hostage-taking scenario or a barricaded suspect, as is the weapons it brings to bear. The typical police motorcycle, the Harley-Davidsons used by the Israeli Police and the BMW bikes used by some other European units, were too bulky and heavy for counter-terrorist duty. For its specific duties, the motorcycle could not carry special bins for equipment that was carried by regular bike cops, nor could it have a flashing light and a siren—all available room on the bike, that also created bulk on the mobile package, were to be removed. For its lightning fast responses to terrorist acts, and its required ability to cut through the narrow avenues and alleyways, the bike had to be as narrow as possible. The only item identifying the motorcycle as a police vehicle, in fact, would be the red and white police license plates that is seen on every police car, from a bomb-squad jeep to a patrol cruiser.

When Commander Amit issued the order to create the Anti-Terrorist Motorcycle Unit, he realized that recruiting officers for this new and unconventional unit might be difficult. The first members of the unit were Jerusalem cops who owned their own motorcycles and were veterans of elite army units. They had to be adept to speed, and to achieve regular high-scores on the range with their machine guns and assault rifles. Soon, however, as the unit expanded from four cops to a force of nearly a dozen and it was decided to place the force within the framework of the Jerusalem Special Patrol Unit, and open the unit solely to *Ya'sa'm* cops. "If it was going to be an elite squad," claims Lieutenant Y.,[*] a member of the unit from day one, "then we needed to fill our ranks with elite cops." The selection process was grueling. The cops had to be expert motorcycle drivers and expert shots. A low score in either the driving or shooting aspect of their selection and training warranted the officer being kicked out of the unit. "There is no room for error in a unit like this," claims Superintendent Rafi Havivyan, the charismatic commander of the Jerusalem *Ya'sa'm*, "this is like the bomb-squad. These cops race at high-speeds and shoot while in motion. If they crash their bikes because of whatever reason or miss whatever they've placed inside their gunsights, they could cause just as much damage as they were sent in to prevent."

Today, the unit consists of thirty police officers and twelve motorcycles. The bike finally selected was the Kawasaki-500 —a

[*] Identity withheld for security reasons.

Prior to an operational deployment on a counter-bombing detail, officers in the Jerusalem Anti-Terrorist Motorcycle Unit prepare for their usual outdoor briefing.

The equipment of the Jerusalem Anti-Terrorist Motorcycle Unit officer is simple—khaki fatigue trousers, black "Police" T-shirt, pistol belt (and Ta'as Jericho 941 9mm pistol), and either a CAR-15 5.56mm assault rifle or, as seen here, a Ta'as Mini-Uzi 9mm submachine gun. The ubiquitous leather jacket and specially modified crash helmet are required elements of the package, as well.

staying alive, and hitting their targets, would solely be the task of the recruits to the new unit. "It wasn't an easy job developing tactics, response procedures and strategies, and tactical safety guidelines," admitted an Anti-Terrorist Motorcycle Unit sergeant, "but after a few minor glitches, we began to gel as a cohesive force that was daring enough to do the job, and trained adequately to get it done effectively and safely. Several officers in the unit were also sent to Turkey for advanced training with their creators of the concept. "

In the spring of 1995, Commissioner Hefetz and Commander Amit unveiled the unit to a small assembly of police officials. At a firing range on the outskirts of the city, the police officers displayed how they could reach a job at high speeds, remove their weapons from special holsters, and then, while the motorcycle was traveling at top speeds and negotiating sharp turns, empty a thirty-round magazine square into the center of a pop-up target. The display was an incredible testament to the hard work that went into creating the unit, and it did something that few displays in Israel ever succeed in accomplishing—it convinced the nay-sayers that the unit had tremendous potential.

In its two years in operation, the Anti-Terrorist Motorcycle Unit has seen more than its share of action. It has responded to armed terrorists moving through the Arab section of the city, driven through the ancient alleyways and streets of the Old City in pursuit of heavily armed suspects, and has been first on the scene after Hamas suicide-bombers blew up three buses and killed nearly fifty civilians. The November 4,

The unit's fleet of Kawasaki-500 and KLEs, including the removable red and white police license plates for potential undercover use.

powerful motorcycle with a liquid-cooled, eight-valve inline-twin engine. A rugged and sleek machine of fine maneuverability, high-speed and comfort, the Kawasaki-500 was also civilian-looking enough where the unit could actually deploy undercover if need be; the Israeli Police, with specialized counter-terrorist undercover units operating in the West Bank, had a long history of having its specialized units operate outside the traditional trappings of uniform. There was talk of painting all the bikes in the blue and white scheme that adorns all Israeli police vehicles (expect those belonging to the Border Guards, which are painted olive drab), but in the end it was decided to leave the Kawasaki-500s in their civilian multi-color scheme. Each officer accepted into the unit underwent a month of advanced driving instruction, from the basic of motorcycle handling, to safely performing a hair-pin turn at ninety miles-per-hour without killing both driver, partner (and possibly any civilian who happened to be nearby). Great emphasis was placed on firearms proficiency as well. While Israeli police officers pride themselves with their weapons skill, there is a difference between emptying a magazine of 9mm full-metal-jackets from an officer's Jericho 941 service automatic to firing three-round bursts of 5.56mm fire from a CAR-15 assault rifle while that same officer is sitting upright on the small bit of remaining cushion, wearing a helmet and visor and flying up and down the streets of the capital at full-speed. The training was rough and dangerous; "Anytime you combine, and I mean combine, high-speeds and the live firing of automatic weapons," an instructor would comment, "you had the possibility of someone getting hurt." Reducing the risk when these officers deployed was the responsibility of the training officers, but

A two-man tandem from the Jerusalem Anti-Terrorist Motorcycle Unit heads to a job in the city's Talpiot neighborhood.

With "regular" motorcycle cops at the ready, and bikes from the Jerusalem Anti-Terrorist Motorcycle Unit only yards away, an Israeli secret service agent monitors security around the Knesset during the swearing in of Prime Minister Benjamin Netanyahu.

1995, assassination of Prime Minister Yitzhak Rabin underscored the need for a police augmentation to the typical *Shin Bet* (the Hebrew acronym for the General Security Service) "package" that usually surrounded the Israeli Prime Minister, government officials, and visiting dignitaries. One of the unit's largest operations was the funeral for Prime Minister Rabin, in which the force was a key element in the massive security umbrella required to safeguard the eighty world leaders who traveled to Jerusalem to pay their respects to the slain Israeli leader; while Anti-Terrorist Motorcycle Unit convoys helped secure the motorcades of American President Bill Clinton and Jordan's King Hussein, other units stood at the ready to key intersections, their weapons at the ready, poised to respond at a moment's notice to any attack. The Anti-Terrorist Motorcycle Unit proved so successful in its abilities that it impressed even *Shin Bet* commanders, especially the desks responsible for VIP and Dignitary Protection. Under a directive issued in the wake of the governmental investigation behind the security lapses that resulted in the killing of Prime Minister Rabin, elements of the Jerusalem *Ya'sa'm* would be transferred to *Shin Bet* command in order to augment existing security details, and help expand and secure the "sterile" area that is needed in the outer perimeter of any VIP and Dignitary protection operation.

Like cops in any elite unit, be it a SWAT unit or the bomb-squad, a unique esprit de corps exists in the Anti-Terrorist Motorcycle Unit. The cops are brash, conceded and, since they ride through the wind with their heavy firepower, they feel invincible. "Even though these guys appear to the outsider to be supermen," admits one of the unit's officers, who is one of the quieter cops hanging out in front of a government office prior to commencing a counter-terrorist detail, "they have developed an outer veil of self-confidence that masks the very dangers they encounter, and the fears on the face, on a daily basis." Mostly, though, the officers in the units are experienced Jerusalem cops who know every inch of the city. On many jobs, as they monitor the city's various frequencies, once they hear an address come over the air they have fired up their engines and are racing at top speed to a location even before the dispatcher has had time to give out the corresponding cross-streets.

Just as the unit has developed a special personality as a collective elite, an even greater relationship exists between partners. The unit operates with steady partners. Unless someone is in court or sick, there are always the same two cops on the bike, although they alternate as to who drive and who commands the team; the "shooter" is always the bike

commander. A closed communication system connects both driver and commander, and a voice-activated radio is placed inside the specially modified crash helmets. For covert messages, when police radios are not to be used, cops in the Anti-Terrorist Motorcycle Unit are all connected to a central paging system, and they all carry cellular phones. The team commander is responsible for communicating with central despatch and with his senior commanders, and the driver's sole task is to negotiate a safe and speedy path for the team. The unit's senior commander selects the two-man tandem based on personality, ability, and experience.

One added bonus of the unit is its anti-crime abilities. During the dress-rehearsal live-fire exhibit put on for the media, the Anti-Terrorist Motorcycle Unit displayed its additional skills at thwarting car-theft and car-jackings, by being able to safely chase suspected vehicles and, with an officer aiming an assault rifle or submachine gun at the driver's window, possess enough deterrence to convince the thief to pull the vehicle over to a quick and uneventful stop. On the streets, however, the unit has scored its greatest success in counter-narcotics operations. In an attempt to help crush the growing narcotics trade connecting Arab East Jerusalem to the Jewish half of the city, Commander Amit despatched the unit to areas where drug sales were rampant. By temporarily removing their red and white license plates in lieu of regular civilian yellow and black ones, the Anti-Terrorist Motorcycle Unit possessed two inherent advantages in operating in locations where criminals and drug gangs ruled the landscape: for a while they were virtually unrecognizable to the perpetrators as being police; and, if a heavily armed drug gang resisted arrest, the unit possessed enough immediate firepower to crush the resistance even before it began. Initial arrests were incredible.

Today, the Anti-Terrorist Motorcycle Unit is deployed not only on patrol, but as tactical back-up to the entire Jerusalem Police force, coming to the aid of street cops when they have encountered problems in dealing with everything from emotionally disturbed persons, to chasing purse snatchers, to keeping order amid the chaos of a bus being blown up by a suicide bomber. The unit has been such a success that similar squads are being planned for Tel Aviv and some of Israel's other large cities. "You can't beat success," a member of the unit told a visiting sergeant from the Atlanta Police Department during an exchange program, "innovation and some well-trained cops can actually work, even in police work." Currently, the Jerusalem Police Anti-Terrorist Unit is being closely studied by departments in Asia, Europe and North America.

A Jerusalem Police bomb-squad truck responds to a suspicious device near the Ministry of Finance.

Following the discovery of a Hamas bomb-house at the eastern fringe of the capital, a bomb-squad truck races toward the call.

The "wings" worn by all Israeli police sappers.

Tel Aviv police sappers examine a piece of drainage pipe mysteriously hooked together to a detonator and some wires.

Another of the special operations Israel Police unit is its force of *Hablanim*—Bomb Disposal Sappers. Considered by many to be the best EOD men in the world—on a professional plane equal to the bomb-disposal officers working in Belfast and Basque country—the sappers are certainly among the world's busiest. Palestinian terrorists have scored considerable success in killing hundreds of civilians with booby-trapped devices disguised as anything from paint-cans to glue bottles, bicycles and watermelons. In 1993, Israel Police Bomb-Disposal Sappers responded to over 50,000 calls from civilians concerning suspicious packages, over 20,000 calls on potential car bombs and conducted nearly 400,000 reconnaissance patrols to search for potential devices. In the good old days when packages with a fuse and a payload of C-4 and nails were left in market places and cinemas, sappers would "handle" the devices through a wide variety of means—from pliers and specialized tools, to robots. Today, however, Palestinian terrorists with a penchant for explosives are no longer content with blowing things up from a safe distance, they are determined to look into the eyes of their victims before detonating a powerful charge of C-4 and blowing themselves and whatever is around them away—recent Hamas bombings of the No. 5 Bus on Dizengoff Street in Tel Aviv, in which twenty-three were killed and nearly seventy wounded illustrates the destructive potential of this phenomenon. To battle the suicide-bomber, the Israel Police has increased its already aggressive public information campaign to teach Israelis to beware of suspicious objects and has increased its aggressive search for the man behind much of the mayhem and carnage.

The other police in Israel is what is known as the "Green Police," consisting of the *Mishmar Ha'Gvul*, Border Guard, and highly specialized units responsible for hostage-rescue, undercover tactical and fugitive apprehension work, and bomb-disposal tasks inside the West Bank. At its inception in 1950, the Border Guard consisted of fewer than 100 men and was a branch of the Israel Defense Forces (IDF). In 1951, the unit was transferred to the national police and reorganized into three territorial squadrons. Serving along Israel's volatile frontiers to this day—as part of a joint security—arrangement with the IDF, the Border Guards have always been a unique force in that they are the sole integrated unit in all of Israel—its personnel are drawn from every social, economic and racial group in the country, including Jews, Bedouins, Druze Muslims and Circassians. This multi-racial make-up of the Border Guards continues to this day, now supplemented by immigrants from the former Soviet Union and Ethiopia, along with Druze, Bedouins and Circassians who are already "third-generation" green berets. Because they were a "police" unit, the Border Guards served in areas where the IDF could not function due to international truce agreements—especially the safeguarding of border settlements from both terrorist attack and agricultural thefts. Always a professional police force, the para-military nature of their work, in 1964 the Border Guards began conscripting eighteen-year-old Israeli teenagers for mandatory military service. Following the 1967 War, when Border Guard security operations in the newly occupied territories expanded, the force was expanded once again

A Border Guard sapper searches the perimeter outside the Knesset for any planted explosives prior to the arrival of Prime Minister Benjamin Netanyahu. Following the assassination of Prime Minister Rabin, Israeli dignitary protection efforts have been extremely proactive.

A Border Guard sapper "handles" a device found near a Jewish settlement on the road from Ramallah.

Undeterred by the threat of the "suspicious package" being booby-trapped, a Border Guard sapper proceeds to examine a device thrown at an Israeli police vehicle.

and divided into brigades. In 1974, when the Horev Commission handed over internal security responsibility inside Israel to the police and Border Guards, the "green police" trained special units for dispersing large-scale demonstrations, commenced security operations at Israel's airports and ports of entry and also created a national hostage-rescue unit. Known by the acronym of *Ya'ma'm,* for *Yechida Mishtartit Meyuchede*t, or Special Police Unit, the *Ya'ma'm* soon became one of the world's busiest—and best—counter-terrorist and hostage-rescue units, participating in hundreds of operations inside Israel and the Occupied Territories. In June 1982, when the Israel Defense Force invaded Lebanon, the Border Guards were sent into the battle-zone to restore public order in southern Lebanon, while the *Ya'ma'm* was sent into the fray as a tactical fugitive hunting force and the tactical arm of the Shin Bet, Israel's domestic counter-terrorist and counter-espionage service. Over fifty Border Guards were killed in Lebanon in two separate bombing incidents at their headquarters in the port city of Tyre.

The Border Guard consists of 5,000 men and has duties as diverse as protecting rural agricultural settlements to mounting joint-security patrols with Palestinian Police units around Jericho and the Gaza Strip. The Border Guards also possess several elite units of their own—including the *Ya'mas*. The *Yechidat Ha'Mista'arvim Shel Mishmar Ha'Gvul* (Border Guard Undercover Unit), better known by its acronym of *Ya'mas*. Created in 1990 to supplement the over-burdened IDF undercover units (Cherry and Samson), the *Ya'mas* soon developed into

the premier IDF undercover unit meant to seize and apprehend the most dangerous terrorist fugitives—as many of these wanted suspects are hardened terrorists, individuals responsible for the killings of dozens, *Ya'mas* units are prepared for any scenario. Initially made up of *Ya'ma'm* volunteers (as was the case of the unit's first commander, Superintendent Eli Avraham who was killed during an attack on a terrorist safe-house), the *Ya'mas* operated throughout the Occupied Territories with ease and complete cover; they dressed as old men, old women, young girls and Hamas fire-branding marchers. According to their commander, Superintendent "N.,"[*] "These men feel as comfortable walking around the casbah of Nablus as they do strolling in Tel Aviv." Superintendent "N." knows of what he speaks. The thirty-seven-year old operator assumed command of the unit following the death of Superintendent Avraham, and before his undercover duties he served for twelve years as an officer in the *Ya'ma'm*. In the operational assignments, the men of the *Ya'mas* are faced with a variety of tactical situations that few units of a similar make-up ever encounter—they must sometimes apprehend and subdue a suspect in the middle of an uncontrollable flow of civilians (some of whom are sometimes armed); know how to fire accurately while on the run or from a moving vehicle; and, display unquestioned courage in light of overwhelming numeric odds. The unit is, however, under very strict orders to use the minimal of firepower in its day-to-day operations

[*] Identity withheld for security reasons.

The "Bambi" robot is readied for some "up-close-and-personal" work with what has been confirmed to be an explosive device.

Wearing protective gear and deploying nerves of steel, a Border Guard sapper readies a disarming device to be applied to a verified Hamas explosive device.

and only fire their weapons if a direct threat to their lives—or the lives of others in the immediate vicinity—exists. Between 1990-1994, the *Ya'mas* was responsible for the apprehension of seventy wanted terrorist fugitives, and the killing of fifty of the most violent and most defiant Hamas terrorists. Trained to be remarkable shots, *Ya'mas* undercover operators favor the Ta'as Mini-Uzi 9mm submachine gun and the CAR-15 5.56mm assault rifle—often an Israeli-modified variant with attached forward pistol grip and attached flashlight. The pistol of choice is the Ta'as Jericho 941 9mm semi-automatic and the Beretta—an old favorite with Israeli military and police units.

The *Ya'mas* is *not* a professional police unit like the *Ya'ma'm*, and unlike IDF elite units who draw their personnel from volunteers who strive to be in the unit and often work hard before conscription to hone their minds and bodies to meet such a unit's exacting standards. *Ya'mas* officers, instead, begin to monitor candidates they feel comfortable with at the Border Guards basic training base, while most eighteen-year-old Israelis are conscripted into the IDF, others are taken directly into the Border Guard and serve their three years of mandatory service in the *Mishmar Ha'Gvul*. During Border Guards basic training, which lasts six months and is an infantry and police regimen, *Ya'mas* commanders begin

A Border Guard Command Car from 21 Company secures a stretch of Hizballah country on Israel's border with Lebanon, near Kibbutz Sassa.

The patch of the National Police Border Guards.

The Border Guard shoulder emblem.

61

to monitor the developments of those individuals who are from Middle East backgrounds, who look like Arabs, and who can converse freely in Arabic. If that policeman is a good "soldier," disciplined though showing initiative, special attention is placed on that individual once the training is complete and they are despatched into the field—primarily for security details in the West Bank and Jerusalem. If he's very good, he is ordered to attend a roundtable of Border Guard officers who, for lack of a better word, volunteer the unknowing policeman into the unit. Most, honored for the privilege, gladly accept, and head to a secret training course that lasts three additional months.

Also supplementing the efforts of the Israeli Police to keep the streets of the cities, as well as the West Bank, free from terrorist attack are police sappers, or bomb-disposal experts, are also among the most experienced in the world. They respond to literally tens of thousands of calls a year throughout the country, handling calls of suspicious packages that sometimes turn out to be nothing but discarded or lost items, but sometimes turn out to be massive explosive devices. A special sapper unit exists in the West Bank, one under Border Guard command, that deals with this problem on a slightly larger scale, at a more fanatic pace, with far more actual devices discovered and handled than the false alarms found inside the Green Line.

As the Ya'sa'm is the "blue" police's back-up, be it in Jerusalem, Tel Aviv or the Galilee, the Border Guards, the "green police," are their back-up. Here, prior to a sweep of suspected terrorist locations in East Jerusalem, Border Guard officers assemble for a tactical assignment.

"Nachshon"
The Israeli Prison Service Special Operations Unit

It's a warm summer's day in southwestern Israel, at a junction just outside the town of Ashqelon, situated within earshot of the Gaza Strip and the Palestinian Autonomy, on the picturesque Mediterranean coast, and the city's ever-gridlocked traffic is about to ground to a virtual halt. Outside the gates of the city's Ashqelon Prison, where some of the most dangerous prisoners in Israel are incarcerated, heavily armed Prison Service officers and policemen are about to move two Hamas bomb-makers to a date with a Jerusalem court at the case of another Hamas terrorist held in a suicide attack that claimed a dozen lives. As the gates of the prison swing open and the convoy of prison vehicles and escort cars makes its way out of the prison's main gate onto the connecting roadway, time stands still in a surreal moment of chaos. As the vehicles bank left, en route to the exit onto the main highway lead toward the Israeli capital, the blinding flash and the deafening blast of a grenade disrupts the routine. Gunmen, wearing masks and carrying assault rifles, rake the lead vehicles of the convoy with magazine-emptying 5.56mm fusillades, while an explosive device is fastened to the rear-cabin where the two terrorists are held in shackles. The plastique rips open the locked compartment and the two bearded men, blindfolded and in their rusty-red prison fatigues, are hurried into a mini-van that screeches to a halt in front of the mayhem.

The terrorists have done their homework, but the Prison Service officers aren't about to let the escape plan reach fruition. The officers, in their characteristic sage green fatigues, deploy from behind the cover of their vehicle and return fire with their Jericho 9mm pistols, and Mini-Uzi submachine guns. As cover fire is laid down with M-16 5.56mm assault rifles, the officers advance in a well-choreographed cadence of swift movement. Moving as fast as they can in a back-breaking crouch, the officers first disable the escape vehicle and then go after the terrorists. The gun-battle is hellatious, but after a protracted three-minute fight, an

The patch of the Israeli Prison Service.

eternity when bullets are flying, the end result is a victory for the good-guys. Not everyone is happy, however. A senior officer, a towering icon of a man with a buzz-cut hairdo and a barrel of a chest, walks out into the smoking mess, carrying a stop-watch, a clipboard and an expression of mild resignation. The ambush was a drill, though the response was a far cry from anything make-believe. In a prison system where a fair majority of the maximum security inmates are terrorists responsible for dozens of cold-blooded killings, nothing is left for chance. The morning fire-fight in Ashqelon didn't take place in Ashqelon, in fact—it was staged at a top-secret training facility for the Israeli Police counter-terrorist team. The terrorists were Israeli police officers as were the two escorted prisoners. The exercise went well—but not perfect and in the business of high-risk corrections security, less than perfect gets people killed. "The terrorists were able to seize the initiative once the firing started," the commander tells his men, "the follow car should have moved here," he continues, "the counter-assault team should have focused on the bad guys and not the prisoners."

For the men of *Nachshon*, the Israeli Prison Service special response team, the morning's festivities have only just begun. Until their commander is completely satisfied, the unit will train, exercises, practice and do everything over again. High-risk escorts, though, is but one facet of *Nachshon*'s operational tasks. It is a unit that has been ground breaking in its application of special warfare know-how and tactics to the world of corrections. It is a unit that, because of a changing Israel and a changing Middle East, finds itself busier than it has ever been before.

There is a total of fifteen correctional facilities and three detention centers throughout the country (those that were once in the Occupied West Bank and Gaza Strip have since been closed). These twenty-two

Nachshon *officers engage one another in a very real training session of Krav-Maga.*

installations are administratively divided among the IPS's three geographic districts: North, South, and Central. Today, there are approximately 10,000 inmates in Israeli prisons, sixty-percent of which are imprisoned for criminal offenses. Of the criminal population, approximately twenty-percent are in prison for drug-related offenses, forty-percent for property-related crimes, and the remainder imprisoned for violent crimes, sexual assault and murder. Forty-percent of the IPS inmates are terrorists in prison serving lengthy terms for shootings, bombings, conspiracy, and other public security related offenses. Recently, the IPS population has been inundated with recent arrivals from the former Soviet Union—ranging from prostitutes and racketeers, to heavy-hitting members of the Georgian and Uzbeki Mafias. The responsibility for securing and maintaining Israel's prisons falls with the 3,500 officers of the IPS—law enforcement officers that carry fire-arms, IPS officers maintain a civil-service ranking similar to that of the Israeli National Police.

In a nation world-known for its daring and innovative approach to being a military underdog in a region beset by enemies, a special operations mentality runs strong throughout Israel's security agencies—including the IPS. Long before prison bureaus in other regions of the world established Special Emergency Response Teams (SERTs) to deal with prison-riots and hostage-taking incidents, the IPS established a small and top-secret force trained to decisively handle the most sensitive, and

sometimes most violent, of incidents. Formed in 1973, "*Nachshon*," Hebrew for "Dashing," was created by the IPS for a very good—and very urgent—reason: there were thousands of well-trained and politically fanatic terrorists languishing in the Israeli penal system and the potential for a large-scale riot or prison take-over, as had been seen in the United States, was of dire concern. Inmates seizing control of a facility on a spasm of violence or the whim of opportunity was one thing—containing hardened political guerrillas, many of whom were trained by the KGB in Eastern Europe was a different beast entirely. "In many ways the reasons behind our beginning was a blessing in disguise," claims Sergeant E.,[*] a *Nachshon* team-leader, "we were raised with the specific purpose of handling uprisings by men who were trained to kill. It required that we be equal, if not better, than most commando units in the army. Once we were operational, however, those skills we developed made us a highly-effective force used in situations where the operation involved inmates who weren't terrorists, and not prone to such violence."

Initially, motivation made up for a lack of manpower and equipment. The IPS was never the most glamorous of the Israeli security agencies, and most army veterans eager to pursue a professional law enforcement career joined either the police or the Shin Bet, Israel's General Security Service. Nevertheless, once word of *Nachshon* leaked out army veterans, many from combat and commando units began to join the IPS solely with the objective of volunteering into *Nachshon*. Today, nearly all of the unit's 100 officers are elite unit veterans from the ranks of the Israel Defense Forces. "We are like any other commando force in the country," claims a *Nachshon* officer readying his gear for a high-risk prisoner transport, "only in our case most people in the country have never heard of us!"

According to Commander E., "*Nachshon*'s main task is to provide the IPS with a solution in situations that no other units in the service can carry out." Officially, though, the unit's primary missions include: anti-riot operations and the rescue of hostages taken in prison uprisings, system-wide intelligence-gathering, and high-risk prisoner transport. Centrally located in the town of Ramle, approximately ten miles

[*] Identity withheld for security reasons.

The Nachshon *wings.*

southeast of Tel Aviv, *Nachshon* teams are on permanent stand-by to respond to the first signs of any prison trouble. The unit is divided into ten teams of ten officers whose equipment, all color-coded per team, is centrally stored and constantly maintained. All *Nachshon* officers are reachable by means of a sophisticated pager and cellular-phone system, and the unit prides itself to be able to respond to any potential problem anywhere in the country in a matter of hours.

Crushing a prison riot is not an easy task. Employing a small arsenal of breaching tools, many of which are Israeli-designed and considered classified, *Nachshon* teams can enter just about any barricaded and fortified area in, what one *Nachshon* team leader calls, "a decisive manner!" If an entrance is barricaded to the point where a dynamic entry would require an elongated period of time then the element of surprise would be lost. Once inside a besieged cell-block, *Nachshon*'s penchant for speed becomes apparent. To neutralize violent inmates, tear-gas canisters are tossed into cells and then plexi-glass shields are placed over the cell openings to prevent the devices from being tossed back out. *Nachshon* deploys standard tear-gas devices, and specially modified grenade-like canisters that bounce around a cell like pinballs gone wild and make it virtually impossible for a prisoner to jump on it and toss it away. When inmates start fires, or throw Molotov cocktails at officers, *Nachshon* team members are trained to deploy tactically while wearing special flame-retardent suits worn usually just by Fire Deptment personnel. Of course, a cell-block take-over involving hostages is an entirely different matter. Anytime a prison tier or cell-block is seized by rioting inmates and hostages are taken, the emotional burden on the officers tasked with the rescue are enormous. The hostages are, like the rescuers, officers of the same prison service. They are brothers in arms and nobody wants to have a job end badly that results in a funeral. As a result, *Nachshon* trains tactically to deploy like a police or military hostage-rescue team. They are expert shots with their Israel Military Industries Jericho 9mm automatics with great proficiency, they train in urban close-quarter combat, and are taught to deploy their skill and judgment in that one spilt-second where a pull on the trigger or a second's hesitation might end with one of their comrades—and buddies—being killed.

"The only guarantee in hostage-rescue work," claims a *Nachshon* officer cleaning his weapon, "is that there is no guarantee. We know that any such situation is dangerous and often desperate. We train, though, to go after the prisoners who are holding weapons and directly threatening the lives of the hostages. Once they are neutralized, either by an order to surrender or by force, and only then can we deploy properly and end a situation. We are not here to kill anyone, and we much rather use some martial arts on a prisoner holding a guard with a razor to his throat or a gun to his head, than a bullet, but we have to respond to the perceived threat and act accordingly." *Nachshon* officers are trained to use deadly force as an absolute and unflinching final option in the execution of their mission. As a result, martial arts and more correctly the Israeli-version of martial arts known as Krav-Maga (or "Contact Fighting"), is taught religiously. Utilizing a common-sense approach to street-fighting rather than a structured routine of moves and gestures, Krav-Maga is a highly aggressive form of no-hold's barred fighting where survival is the only

sign of victory—anything and everything, from eye-scratching to biting off an opponents fingers, is permitted. Krav-Maga instruction is a large-part of the *Nachshon* training regimen. "We aren't necessary very large," claims a 5'8" officer who owns the reputation as being the unit's top fighter, "but once the inmates see how we can handle a man twice our size, they think twice the next time they might want to start trouble."

Unlike other SERT teams in North America, *Nachshon* is not solely a reactionary force. If a warden feels that the prisoners of a particular block are planning a large-scale disturbance, a major drug transaction or, in the worst-case scenario, a prison break, he will despatch *Nachshon* teams into cell-blocks to, in the words of one *Nachshon* supervisor, "Disrupt the normalcy and security of prisoner life." *Nachshon* is routinely despatched into the system's prisons to search for hidden weapons, drugs and other intelligence material that might help uncover a major plan for a disturbance or an escape. Additional intelligence-gathering methods, such as visual surveillance, are also employed. The IPS also deploys another "specialized unit" to check on existing security arrangements currently operational in IPS facilities in what the service calls "an aggressor role." Dressed as convicts, the officers will test electronic and visual censors, test gates, locks and dead areas, and submit reports recommending improvements.

A Nachshon officer demonstrates the flame-retardent suit worn by unit officers during prison disturbances.